Editor-in-Chief and Founder:
Lyndon H. LaRouche, Jr.
Editorial Board: *Lyndon H. LaRouche, Jr. , Helga Zepp-LaRouche, Robert Ingraham, Tony Papert, Gerald Rose, Dennis Small, Jeffrey Steinberg, William Wertz*
Co-Editors: *Robert Ingraham, Tony Papert*
Technology: *Marsha Freeman*
Transcriptions: *Katherine Notley*
Ebooks: *Richard Burden*
Graphics: *Alan Yue*
Photos: *Stuart Lewis*
Circulation Manager: *Stanley Ezrol*

INTELLIGENCE DIRECTORS
Economics: *Marcia Merry Baker, Paul Gallagher*
History: *Anton Chaitkin*
Ibero-America: *Dennis Small*
Russia and Eastern Europe: *Rachel Douglas*
United States: *Debra Freeman*

INTERNATIONAL BUREAUS
Bogotá: *Miriam Redondo*
Berlin: *Rainer Apel*
Copenhagen: *Tom Gillesberg*
Lima: *Sara Madueño*
Melbourne: *Robert Barwick*
Mexico City: *Gerardo Castilleja Chávez*
New Delhi: *Ramtanu Maitra*
Paris: *Christine Bierre*
Stockholm: *Ulf Sandmark*
United Nations, N.Y.C.: *Leni Rubinstein*
Washington, D.C.: *William Jones*
Wiesbaden: *Göran Haglund*

ON THE WEB
e-mail: eirns@larouchepub.com
www.larouchepub.com
www.executiveintelligencereview.com
www.larouchepub.com/eiw
Webmaster: *John Sigerson*
Assistant Webmaster: *George Hollis*
Editor, Arabic-language edition: *Hussein Askary*

———

EIR (ISSN 0273-6314) *is published weekly (50 issues), by EIR News Service, Inc., P.O. Box 17390, Washington, D.C. 20041-0390. (703) 297-8434*

European Headquarters: E.I.R. GmbH, Postfach Bahnstrasse 9a, D-65205, Wiesbaden, Germany
Tel: 49-611-73650
Homepage: http://www.eir.de
e-mail: info@eir.de
Director: Georg Neudecker

Montreal, Canada: 514-461-1557
eir@eircanada.ca

Denmark: EIR - Danmark, Sankt Knuds Vej 11, basement left, DK-1903 Frederiksberg, Denmark.
Tel.: +45 35 43 60 40, Fax: +45 35 43 87 57. e-mail: eirdk@hotmail.com.

Mexico City: EIR, Sor Juana Inés de la Cruz 242-2 Col. Agricultura C.P. 11360
Delegación M. Hidalgo, México D.F.
Tel. (5525) 5318-2301
eirmexico@gmail.com

Canada Post Publication Sales Agreement #40683579

Postmaster: Send all address changes to *EIR*, P.O. Box 17390, Washington, D.C. 20041-0390.

Signed articles in *EIR* represent the views of the authors, and not necessarily those of the Editorial Board.

After Helsinki

With the Conclusion of the Schiller Institute Conference

EIR Contents

www.larouchepub.com   Volume 45, Number 28, July 13, 2018

Helsinki.

ZEPP-LAROUCHE WEBCAST

Schiller Institute Conference Leads Way For Europe to Enter the New Paradigm!

This is the edited transcript of the July 5, 2018 Schiller Institute New Paradigm webcast, an interview with the founder of the Schiller Institutes, Helga Zepp-LaRouche. She was interviewed by Harley Schlanger. A video *of the webcast is available.*

Harley Schlanger: Hello, I'm Harley Schlanger. Welcome to our weekly webcast of the Schiller Institute featuring our founder and Chairwoman Helga Zepp-LaRouche.

Last weekend, the Schiller Institute convened a profoundly successful conference in Bad Soden, Germany, around the theme of the memo by Helga Zepp-La-Rouche, calling for the application of the "Singapore model"—referring to the summit between President Trump and President Kim Jong-un—as a model for all international relations. The conference included speakers from many nations, including Russia and China, from Africa, Europe, and the United States. More than 300 participants engaged in a very lively back and forth dialogue for the two full days of the weekend.

Helga, by all measures, this was a highly successful conference. Are you satisfied that it accomplished the objective you set out for it?

Overcoming Seemingly Impossible Differences

Helga Zepp-LaRouche: Yes. I think the participants all expressed a profound optimism that with the ideas presented, a solution can be found. And everyone noted what distinguishes the Schiller Institute from other organizations; other organizations have conferences, sometimes on specific subjects, with experts who deliver PowerPoint presentations, but their audiences aren't elevated to the level of thinking required to find solutions. That was why I called my presentation "The Coincidence of Opposites," *coincidentia oppositorum*, an idea of Nicholas of Cusa. It's a specific way of thinking about how to overcome the contradictions of political discourse and interaction. If you just look at the status quo, you will never be able to find a solution.

The main subject of this conference was how the New Silk Road can be applied to the African and Southwest Asian refugee crisis. There were several panels;

EIRNS/Christopher Lewis

Roger Stone addressing the conference by video.

first a strategic panel which was extremely interesting, in which there were top speakers from government-related think tanks from China and Russia, who represented their viewpoint on the difficulties and opportunities of the New Silk Road. A highlight of that panel was Roger Stone, speaking by live video on "The President Trump Europeans Don't Know." Many people in the audience were shocked, but also they said, "Well, I had to agree with every word he was saying." So this was very efficient. Then we had former military men from Germany and France, and Virginia State Senator Richard Black, who set the record straight on U.S. policy with respect to Syria.

I think this was a very important introduction to the whole conference. The audience began to understand why we insist that to understand the world picture, you have to put yourself in the shoes of each different country, you have to look at the world the way it looks from China, Russia, the United States, the European countries, Africa and Asia in order to get a more balanced view and be able to form your own judgment, and not be dependent on the fake news from some random media.

Then we had a huge, very successful panel on the development of Africa, with an African ambassador and African specialists talking about the different projects, such as Transaqua and the development perspective made possible by Chinese investments in Africa.

Punctuated by a Wonderful Concert

We had a wonderful concert, in which the conductor, in my view quite successfully, attempted to replicate the conducting method of Wilhelm Furtwängler. So this was quite an experience. Videos will soon be available.

Then on the second day, we had the New Silk Road perspective for Europe, with a focus on the Balkans. We had a highly interesting discussion on the importance of higher energy flux-densities and nuclear energy. There was a very important presentation on how to restore international law, which has been abandoned so many times in the recent period.

You may have more to add Harley; I think this conference was very, very timely, because it occurred at the same time as the government crisis in Germany, in which Germany is trying, quite unsuccessfully, to find a solution to the refugee crisis.

I encourage everyone to go to the Schiller Institute site and watch the presentations, and spread them! This is something which really is important for many more people to know about.

Schlanger: The first and second panels are already posted on the Schiller Institute website's homepage, http://www.newparadigm.schillerinstitute.com. I would add that a subtheme of the conference was the point you've made since the beginning of the year, that this should be the year in which we end geopolitics, the practice of pitting nations against one another in a zero-sum, law-of-the-jungle way. Both the Russian speaker and others in their own ways presented their ideas as to how this could work. Our viewers would certainly benefit greatly from discovering, that regardless of where people are from, there is a desire to move into the New Paradigm.

You mentioned the German crisis. There's a lot to talk about. We're now in the "post-Singapore summit" diplomatic period. Let's start with what we just heard Tuesday: U.S. Secretary of State Mike Pompeo is going to be going to North Korea today. On Tuesday, Pompeo spoke with Russian Foreign Minister Sergey Lavrov. There's a density of diplomatic activity under way, isn't there?

Zepp-LaRouche: Yes. The head of the North American Department of the Russian Foreign Ministry yesterday said that the summit is expected to have an "ambitious" agenda, to be very rich, and that the discussions will be extensive. Among the subjects to be discussed, besides Syria, will be the need to have strategic disarmament, the need to have a new INF [Intermediate-Range Nuclear Forces] Treaty, a renewal of the START Treaty, and improvement of the bilateral relations between the United States and Russia.

The Upcoming Putin-Trump Summit

So, even before it has even taken place, judging by the hysteria on the side of the British media, who are talking about this summit in apocalyptic terms, the summit should be very good. Whenever the *Economist* and the *Financial Times* have such fits, then the subject they are discussing is usually something good happening in the world.

In this situation if the United States and Russia can improve relations, which is of paramount importance. In line with the successful Singapore summit, signs indicate that the Helsinki summit could be a similar, breakthrough for the world situation. I think we can be happy that this summit is going to take place.

Schlanger: The European Union just convened a summit last week, supposedly to address the immigration crisis. You had some very sharp comments on this in your conference presentation, so I'd like you to give our viewers today a sense of what you thought happened with this EU summit, and then the alternative— we see the Italians and the Austrians responding at some level to your initiative.

Zepp-LaRouche: Yes, that's the good news, that there are some countries which at least as a tendency, are going in the direction we have been proposing, unlike the German government, which really presented a *terrible* picture! You had a knives-out fight between Chancellor Angela Merkel and [Interior Minister] Horst Seehofer. The so-called compromise they reached on the transit centers for refugees at the Bavarian-Austrian border, is already being rejected by many, including the police trade union that said the plan is not workable because it is only about one border, not all the borders.

There is no love between these Christian parties [the CDU of Merkel and Bavaria-based CSU of Seehofer]. Considering the way they have treated each other, no matter what compromise was reached between Merkel and Seehofer, they were so mean to each other and so nasty, that I think this is a now deep crisis of confidence, which will not go away.

And then, the government coalition party, the SPD, the Social Democratic Party, is in a very difficult situation, because if they agree to these transit centers, which they had rejected in 2015, if they capitulate to this compromise, which is really Merkel's capitulation to Seehofer, then the SPD can be expected to drop more in the polls. In any case, many expect this coalition government will not last to the end of its term.

German Government Crisis

There was for a short period a "coalition of the willing" among the Italians, the Austrians, and Seehofer on the refugee question, but now this too is falling apart. Seehofer went to Vienna today and was told that there will be no solution at the expense of Austria. If Seehofer closes the Bavarian border with Austria, Austria will close its border with Italy, and there will be a jam up of refugees.

That demonstrates that any effort to solve the problem within the existing old paradigm, will not reach a

cc/Harald Bischoff

Horst Seehofer (left) with German Chancellor Angel Merkel.

solution. There is complete disunity in the EU with strong dissent from the Visegrad countries, the Balkan countries, and the South Europeans. There was a huge freak-out in the *Financial Times* two days ago, accusing the new "strongman" in Italy, [Lega leader and Deputy Prime Minister] Matteo Salvini, of detonating the EU— complaining that Salvini no longer accepts the French-German dictatorship over Europe—so you have complete disarray.

That is why we have been proposing that this problem must be approached in a completely different way. Even though we discussed this last week, let me just repeat: We want the European countries (I think the EU is unlikely to do it) to invite President Xi Jinping and African leaders to a summit, which could then establish a crash program for the extension of the New Silk Road into Africa.

A Huge Endeavor

This is a huge endeavor, but if three or four really big infrastructure projects are chosen, combined with an intention to build up the infrastructure of Africa in a crash effort, this would get things going. The presence of President Xi Jinping would add tremendous credibility to the intention of industrializing Africa with Chinese help. Such an initiative would provide a great incentive for the young people and others who are now fleeing from hunger and epidemics, or perhaps thinking of doing so in the future, to re-integrate themselves in building up the African economies.

In this way, we would end the refugee crisis by doing what Franklin D. Roosevelt did with the New Deal, in which he also integrated the youth into that nation's economy, initially through the CCC program. Youth learned quickly, on the job, and in the end, became the skilled labor force of an industrial revolution.

This is the approach that has to be taken. Chancellor Sebastian Kurz of Austria announced an EU Summit with Africa, to take place this year, during the time that Austria holds the EU presidency. So this is very good. In September, there will be a big conference between China and the African Union [the third summit of the Forum on China-Africa Cooperation (FOCAC)], and that will set a certain standard. We will keep pushing this idea, even beyond the present EU summit. I did not expect that this EU summit would do what was required, but nevertheless it would have been the correct policy. It remains the correct policy; therefore, we will keep organizing for it.

Refugee Crises

The refugee crises, not only between Africa and Europe, but also between Latin America and the United States, need this approach. The countries which the refugees are coming from need to be developed; it's the only human way. In Mexico, there is now some hope that things may go in this direction, because the newly elected President, Andrés Manuel López Obrador, said that he had a very good telephone discussion with President Trump discussing great projects in Mexico, creating many jobs, and that way, Mexico could help to reduce the refugee crisis for the United States. So this is the way to go, but we need more of it. Everyone listening can help.

Schlanger: I can report from the sidelines of our conference that there was great enthusiasm from the Europeans, the Russians, the Chinese and the Africans, to this approach. The question they kept coming back to was, "How do we do it, given the existing institutions?" One of the interesting points you made in the discussion session with one of these officials was that the existing institutions are barely surviving. The opportunity exists now to establish new institutions.

On that note—the instability of the EU—there was just a fairly interesting visit by the Polish Prime Minister to the European Parliament in Strasbourg. What happened?

Polish Prime Minister Mateusz Morawiecki (right), with Frans Timmermans, First Vice-President of the European Commission.

Zepp-LaRouche: That meeting makes clear what a low point this EU has reached in relations with its member states. First of all, Polish Prime Minister Mateusz Morawiecki was completely snubbed. EU Commission President Jean-Claude Juncker didn't go to greet him; his first deputy Frans Timmerman didn't go either. Instead a lower level commissioner was dispatched to receive him and escort him to the plenary assembly.

Poland

Then he was attacked by MEP Manfred Weber, who heads the Christian Democratic bloc (the European People's Party) in the European Parliament, who was very provocative: "What happened to the Polish media? There is only propaganda. Why do you only arrest peaceful demonstrators and not the right wing?" Although clearly upset with that, Morawiecki replied that he didn't think the EU Commission or the EU is any longer an honest mediator with Poland. So that relationship is obviously at a low point. And the situation between Italy and France is at a low point. So I think the EU does not look in good shape at all.

Schlanger: One interesting development in an EU country—you mentioned Austria—in Vienna, the Vienna Institute for International Economic Studies (WIIW) just put out a very positive report about Europe joining the New Silk Road. We've seen some motion in this direction in Vienna. Do you think this, in conjunction with the Austrian chairmanship of the European Council, can put this on the agenda of the EU now?

Zepp-LaRouche: I'm sure. Because remember, in the coalition treaty of the new Austrian government, they have a chapter on why Austria wants to become a hub for the New Silk Road. Austria's Transport Minister, Norbert Hofer, has just been in China in April, during which he and the Chinese signed an agreement of understanding that not only should the Eastern European countries be participating in the New Silk Road, but that this is a policy which would benefit the entire economic sphere of the European Union, and that Austria will be the main pusher and mover for this policy.

Austria

That's very good, and the proposal you mentioned from the Vienna Institute for International Economic Studies, proposed that Europe should create its own fund of one trillion euro over the next ten years, with two major corridors: One going from Lisbon to Madrid to Lyon, I think all the way on the one side to Constanta in Romania, and also to Nizhny Novgorod, and Baku—I don't know the routes. I think the proposal is very good. The authors say this will create seven million new jobs in Europe, building railways, bridges, ports, highways, other integrated infrastructure along two possible main routes of a "European Silk Road" that would connect the western European industrial centers with the eastern part of the continent. In total, they encompass a route of 11,000 km.

So I'm very happy, because the more this kind of discussion about investment in the real economy and infrastructure occurs, the more those people who are not completely evil or stupid will benefit from this discussion. I'm absolutely sure this discussion will eventually reach every European country. The New Paradigm cooperation for the benefit of each other, for win-win cooperation, is the spirit of the time, the New Silk Road Spirit. I think it's very good that Austria has now the Presidency of the EU until the end of the year,

and I think Chancellor Kurz is quite the energetic man to put this on the agenda. This is very good.

Schlanger: Helga, there was a very significant development coming out of Kyiv, Ukraine concerning Natalia Vitrenko, a good friend of yours and the Schiller Institute. The Progressive Socialist Party of Ukraine (PSPU), which she chairs, has been illegally kept off the ballot since 2010. The Schiller Institute conducted an international mobilization, and one of our friends, European Parliament Member Marco Zanni—who spoke at our conference this last weekend—intervened with the EU foreign affairs high representative Federica Mogherini, asking her how can the EU sit by when these political parties are being suppressed in Ukraine? Yesterday, a court ruled that it was illegal to keep her party off the ballot.

This is a significant development: What do you make of this in terms of a potential to shift the situation in Ukraine?

EIRNS/Daniel-Enrico Grasenack-Tente

Dr. Natalia Vitrenko addressing a Schiller Institute Conference in Germany in 2013.

Ukraine, Natalia Vitrenko

Zepp-LaRouche: Well, Natalia Vitrenko is a foremost economist, she is an extremely well educated stateswoman, and she has a program of integrating Ukraine into the New Silk Road. She spoke at our previous conference about the subject and this is indeed creating an alternative. Ukraine is a country which is in the west Catholic and pro-West, and in the east, Orthodox and pro-Russian. Unfortunately there are a lot of Nazi elements in the picture. Because the only way to solve the very dicey problem of Ukraine—which is still a potential trigger for a larger war—is by integrating Europe, the EU (or European nations), and the Eurasian Economic Union (EAEU), with the New Silk Road, the Belt and Road Initiative.

If you go back to this idea of a single integrated Eurasian continent, from Lisbon to Vladivostok, which will clearly benefit from this economic joint development, I think a peaceful solution can be found to the Ukraine problem. And Natalia Vitrenko, I'm sure, will campaign on that issue, and that is a hopeful sign, not only for Ukraine, but actually for all of us.

Schlanger: I'd like to conclude by coming back to the Schiller Institute Conference, and again, to remind our viewers to go the New Paradigm Schiller Institute website, where the first day's two panels are already up. One of the underlying themes, I guess you would say, of the conference, was the recognition of the role that you've played—but also the role of your husband, Lyndon LaRouche—over the past four to five decades. Many people were probably surprised—pleasantly surprised—to hear Roger Stone, who identified himself as 40-year friend of Donald Trump, and who I would argue was the architect of Trump's election campaign victory, praise Lyn's visionary ideas.

EIRNS/Christopher Lewis

A concert of Classical music was presented on June 30, after the first two panels of the June 30-July 1 conference in Bad Soden, Germany.

Law, Lawfulness and International Law

In the discussion period, you mentioned international law, and a very useful discussion ensued about where law comes from. So maybe you have a couple of more thoughts on that.

Zepp-LaRouche: Yes. We had a very excellent presentation by Prof. Hans Köchler, president of the International Progress Organization in Vienna, who discussed what we have to do to either reform the UN or make it function, by addressing the fact that the very setup of the Permanent Five in the Security Council is something which came out of the historic situation in the aftermath of World War II, but which must now be replaced.

Another very important idea was that, in the future world which many nations are involved in building, the new order must be based on principles, not only like the Human Rights Declaration of 1948, which is the closest approximation to what the new order should be.

In many countries of the world, discussions are taking place that we have to give ourselves—as a human species—an order more in correspondence with the lawfulness of the physical universe, that only the idea of continuous change and an anti-entropic universe can give us such a guideline to inform our political life, and that the only people who are capable of thinking in this way are the scientists, and artists of Classical culture, because only they are used to thinking in terms of universal principles, which are repeatable and therefore valid, and therefore beyond the realm of opinion, but related to the deeper, underlying truth of the lawfulness of our universe.

Take the Standard of the American Revolution

Obviously, this is a very deep philosophical discussion. It requires that many nations of the world—preferably all of them—be involved in this discussion, because we want to arrive at something binding, in a certain sense, on the level of the discussion of the *Federalist Papers* after the American Revolution, but this time on a world level. We need to be discussing how to provide ourselves with an order which allows self-governance and the living of human beings together. And that must be applied today on an international level. How can we make sure that we do not plunge into dark ages again, by simply elevating our populations to think in terms of a New Paradigm of the coincidence of opposites, of the one humanity first, or what Xi Jinping always calls "a community of a shared humanity," or "shared future of mankind."

So I think that is a discussion I would invite all of you, our viewers and listeners, to engage in with us. Become a member of the Schiller Institute! Help us to spread the knowledge about the need for New Paradigm thinking, and joint efforts with us.

Schlanger: Well, Helga, thank you very much. And to all our viewers, you now have your marching orders! Let's see if you can follow through on them. So, until next week, we'll see you again.

Schiller Institute Conference
Bad Soden, June 30-July 1, 2018

The Urgent Need for a New Paradigm in International Relations
A Peace Order Based on the Development of Nations

SATURDAY, JUNE 30*

10:00 – CONFERENCE KEYNOTE: **The Coincidence of Opposites—The World of Tomorrow**
Helga Zepp-LaRouche, Chairwoman of the Schiller Institute

Panel I

How to Overcome Geopolitics and the Danger of a New World War

- Russia's Role in the New World Order
  Vladimir Morozov, Program Coordinator, Russian International Affairs Council, Moscow

- Globalization in Reverse and the Challenge for China's Foreign Policy in the New Era
  Dr. Xu Jian, Vice President of China Institute of International Studies (CIIS), Director of CIIS Academic Council, and Senior Research Fellow

- The True Interest of the United States
  U.S. State Senator Richard Black (video presentation)

- Interest Monsters: Democracy, Human Rights and Other Hypocrisies
  Lt. Col. (ret.) Ulrich Scholz, former NATO planner

The two panels of the second day of the conference, held on July 1, 2018, are covered in this issue—July 13—of EIR. The two panels of the first day of the conference—June 30, 2018—were covered in last week's issue of EIR, dated July 6, 2018.

- The U.S. Refusal of a Multipolar World Makes the Transition Very Painful
  Colonel (ret.) Alain Corvez, International Consultant, former Counsellor for the French Defense and Interior Ministries

- The President Trump Europeans Do Not Know
  Roger Stone, U.S. Political Strategist of the Trump Faction in the Republican Party (live video presentation)

Panel II

How the Belt and Road Initiative Is Changing Africa: The Only Human Solution to the Refugee Crisis

- Opening Remarks
  Hussein Askary, Southwest Asia Coordinator of the Schiller Institute

- A Role for Europe in the Belt and Road Initiative
  Wang Hao, Embassy of the People's Republic of China to the Federal Republic of Germany, 1st Secretary for Economy and Trade

- After the Transaqua Breakthrough, Nigeria Comes to the Fore
  H.E. Yusuf Maitama Tuggar, Ambassador of the Federal Republic of Nigeria to Germany

- The Impact of Transaqua on the Future Development of Africa
  Mohammed Bila, Expert Modeler, Lake Chad Basin Observatory, Lake Chad Basin Commission

- What Pan-Africanism on the Silk Road?
  Amzat Boukari-Yabara, African Historian, General Secretary of the Pan-African League—UMOJA

- Challenges for Peace and Reconstruction in Yemen
  Representatives of the Yemeni Association Insan for Human Rights and Peace

- Operation Felix: Yemen's Reconstruction and Connection to the Belt and Road
  Hussein Askary, Southwest Asia Coordinator for the Schiller Institute

Greetings to the Conference *from Prof. Michele Geraci, newly appointed Undersecretary of State in the Ministry for Economic Development, Italy*

20:00 – CONCERT OF CLASSICAL MUSIC

Sunday, July 1

Panel III

The Future of European Nations—Cultural and Economic Grand Design within the New Paradigm

- KEYNOTE: **Europe's Future Needs to Be Inclusive, with the New Silk Roads and the World Land-Bridge**
  Jacques Cheminade, President of Solidarité et Progrès, France

- The Re-establishment of International Law
  Prof. Hans Köchler, President of Iternational Progress Organisation

- Has European Integration Gone Too Far?
  Marco Zanni, Member of the European Parliament from Italy

- The Controllable Energy
  Dr. Armin Azima, University of Hamburg

Panel IV

Economic and Political Potentials of the One Belt One Road

- How Eastern and South-Eastern Europe Can Participate in Creating a New Global Economic Miracle
  Elke Fimmen, Schiller Institute

- The New Paradigm from the View of the Balkans
  Prof. Ivo Christov, Member of Bulgarian Parliament

- The Options for Integration of the Eurasian Customs and Economic Union and China's OBOR Initiative
  Folker Hellmeyer, Economist, Germany

- On the New Silk Road—Achievements and Prospects of Economic Cooperation between Serbia and China
  Dusko Dimitrijevic, Ph.D., Professorial Fellow, Institute of International Politics and Economics, Serbia

- Necessary Regulatory Framework for Investments of German and European SME Economy in National Economies along the New Silk Road
  Hans von Helldorff, Spokesman, Federal Association of the German Silk Road Initiative

- The Eurasia Canal and the New Silk Road
  Professor Nuraly Bekturganov, Vice President of Academy of Natural Sciences of Kazakhstan

- The Integration of the Eurasian Continent
  Leonidas Chrysanthopoulos, former Ambassador of Greece, former Secretary General of the Black Sea Economic Cooperation Organization (BSEC)

18:00 – END OF CONFERENCE

JACQUES CHEMINADE

Europe's Future Must Be Inclusive with New Silk Roads and World Land-Bridge

Jacques Cheminade was the first speaker on Panel III of the Schiller Institute conference, on July 1, 2018. He is the leader of Solidarité et Progrès, *the LaRouche movement in France. This is an edited transcript.*

Let's be clear. The European Union has become a walking shadow, a moral corpse. In Italian, you may say a *"morto qui parla."* But it would be self-destructive to fall into a state of morose self-indulgence, into the comfort of blaming ourselves. Second to the British Empire, pessimism is our main enemy, because it paralyses our will. Beyond all criticism, there is the idea and the contribution of Europe to human civilization, which is absolutely different and opposed to the European Union. It is a Europe of the nations, a multiple having generated a one, an immortal contribution to humanity that the world needs.

Our task is to awaken such a Europe from its present nightmare, to bring it out from the Valley of the Clueless where it stagnates and turn it into a new beacon of hope illuminating the world's silk roads. De Gaulle did not fear to say that the princess of the legends, France, should be mobilized to build the European cathedral. But, for real and as a metaphor, a cathedral is not a closed shop, it is a landmark for all those who are outside and a place to conceive of, and pray and work hard for a better world for those who enter.

We are far from that—but, because of the world sit-

Jacques Cheminade

uation and our own, we are not allowed to lose. To win, we first have to look inward and from above, make an examination of conscience—a joyful examination of conscience—because to reach above our state of mind towards the needed relatively higher states will free us from the shackles of impotence and recover our self-esteem.

Let's Arise from our European Waterloo

Let's commit ourselves to arise from the mud of our European Waterloo. For more than thirty years, our leaders have neither responded to the demands of their peoples nor met the challenges of the international situation. As a result, we are withdrawing from change and engaging in a process of balkanization, of decomposition of our identity. We have submitted ourselves to the Empire of the City of London and Wall Street, letting them ruin ourselves and our neighbors in Africa and the Middle East, and then blaming the human beings escaping from those places ruined by our policies, for our misfortunes and woes.

What hypocrisy! At the last European Council of June 28 and 29, our leaders reduced the question of migrants to a thing in itself, trying to transfer to their partners what all see as a burden without the least commitment to a minimum solidarity. Some want to assemble migrants for control in hotspots located in European countries; others want to sub-contract the problem to the countries where the migrants are coming from; all are unable to conceive anything but hotspots, which are nothing but human triage camps, rather than treating the real causes of migrations. Our leaders throw statistics and figures at each other's faces, reducing human lives to accounting evaluations.

Italy had to abandon *Mare nostrum* at the end of 2014, which was the relatively best humanitarian operation organized by a State, because of the absolute lack of European support. All

UNHCR/I. Pavicevic

Refugees at the Tovarnik train station in Croatia, waiting for transportation to a refugee camp near Zagreb.

ended up delegating the job to the NGOs and now blame them as accomplices of the smugglers. With that logic of blame, European ports have been closed to ships carrying the migrants, but in truth, it is all the European leaders that have to be blamed for the criminal inaction of their countries.

I first decided to raise this moral issue because a union of states in which no member considers migrations as a challenge to be solved through massive help in favor of the countries where the migrants are coming from, and where no state organizes itself properly to receive those that come as a potential for the future, is a union that has lost its mandate from Heaven, as the Chinese would say.

The Failed Finite Lifeboat

All European nations share a geopolitical conception of our planet as being a relatively finite universe, a sort of lifeboat which has a limited space to contain a growing population. That is, indeed, the real problem of the European Union: It does not produce real wealth, it does not produce children, and does not welcome foreigners, because it has accepted the rule of a zero-sum universe, a sort of fortress Europa against the people, but friendly to financial speculation, with a euro that has become the conveyor belt for that speculation.

The European reformers and the so-called populists alike, with a few exceptions, are trying to solve a problem within the terms that have created the problem. None faces the cause, which are the policies of the British Empire, Wall Street and the City of London. Macron has exhibited an oratory talent at France's Sorbonne University or in Greece, but only dealing with words and not with reality.

He calls for a "refoundation of Europe," but within the realm of financial liberalism. He was not capable of endorsing a Glass-Steagall Act when he had the opportunity to do so as adviser and later Finance Minister to Hollande, nor today, even though at least some of the Italian ministers and many of their advisers are calling for it. Macron pretends to be a lead climber, but in reality he's begging for German money to be able to climb, while Angela Merkel messes around with her government and covers up for financial interests which all, like the Deutsche Bank, are potentially bankrupt. Others go in all directions, with no vision. None has the courage to see beyond its own nostrils.

Xinhua/Shan Yuqi

German Chancellor Angela Merkel (R) with French President Emmanuel Macron in Berlin, May 15, 2017.

So how can we, here, be morally and culturally optimistic? Because, if we look beyond our terrible state of affairs, since September 2013 there has been a new development: A new model for relations among major powers has been set forth, the model of the new silk roads. This model is based on the principle of absolute respect for the sovereignty of others; it is a new world order based on mutual trust and benefit. The intention, expressed by Chinese Foreign Minister Wang Yi, is to transcend the outdated concepts, such as the clash of civilizations, the Cold War, to go beyond the mere thinking in the geometry of zero-sum games or exclusive clubs. It is precisely the model that should inspire us in Europe today.

Beyond the Liberal Financial Model

Emmanuel Macron, during his January trip to China, said in his Xi'an speech that "we have reached times where France and China can afford to dream together"; reached a point at which "the new silk roads reactivate a collective imagination, an imagination to be shared." Well said, but typical of present European ways, he tries to locate this momentum within a liberal financial model. I would say these are the prison bars of his ideology. There you have a clinical example of today's European failed state of mind: trying to put a nightingale in a cage.

Totally contrary is the Chinese concept of *tianxia*, expanded by Confucius and Mencius, which inspires the policies of Xi Jinping, establishing that when something new comes from outside, it should be adopted inside with an approach which is neither that of an exclusive club nor of a closed shop which adds something without a change, but with a dynamic motion creating the conditions for a higher level of coexistence. "Politics is not, as some would believe, domination by mere force, but the art to create a global cooperation." It is therefore not uniformisation or domination, but what is called in Chinese philosophical terms: "complementarity" with the qualities of inclusiveness, connectivity and attractiveness. Ah, some would say, there you come with an Asian model. Are you sure it will fit for Europe? The answer is no, not only for Europe, it would fit for the whole world.

Tianxia

Why am I so sure? because our great European philosopher, Leibniz, understood it. He wrote, in his *Novissima Sinica*, and in various letters to his Jesuit friends, that the concept of "social harmony" from the Chinese would enrich European culture! The opportunity was missed then, sabotaged by the feudal oligarchy and the British financiers, but it has left marks, footsteps in our Europe. Interestingly, the concept of "complementarity" meets the Leibnizian one of "completedness"—not a destructive uniformization but a mutually harmonious inspiration. For the West today, it is evidently difficult to grasp this new dynamic of the silk

Xinhua

President Macron and First Lady at the Forbidden City, Beijing, Jan. 10, 2018.

roads. The truth is that Europe, as reflected in the question of the migrants, is trapped in the old paradigm of geopolitics and the so-called "free and fair" competition, something which in reality has never existed.

In a provocative book titled, *The Rape of Europe*, Robert Salais, a French historian, describes how right from the beginning, the European Union was under the double rule of free trade and, worse, financial liberalization against the very conception of sovereign nation states. This is my point: Europe should be freed from this financial and ideological cage, as exemplified by the case of Macron and almost all European leaders. We could say that Europe has to be freed from such an original sin that is promoted more and more with a vindictive proselytism absolutely opposed to the Confucian and Leibnizian notion of harmony.

The European Union, in other terms, is not a harmonious union, but an inductive/deductive construct, based on codes, standards and rules that they call "instructions"; it is based on fixed categories, and as such, bound to self-destroy, fading into nothing for lack of creativity. Not destroyed by others, but by its own anti-creative axioms, its mental closedness. I see today's European Union as an endless set of polygons (France calls itself a Hexagon), unable to get to the superior order of the circle that Cusa described, each polygon seeing itself as the reality, or pretending to be the circle; each seeing itself as a oneness, unable to understand the superior principle of rotation which creates the circle.

Beethoven's Harmony, Not Cacophony

What angers me the most is to see a counter-culture expanding everywhere, banalizing human perceptions and appetites, from ultra-violent video games to the imbecility of the "world music." The worst example is what Macron organized on the steps of the Elysée Palace to celebrate the "Day of Music" on June 21. He who pretends to like philosophy and the pomp and riches of the Court, invited a bunch of DJ stars who transformed the Palace in a giant night club where they "sang" such things as "come, come to dance, you motherfucker" and "Let's burn this house tonight, let's burn it from top down" or "shit everywhere, she was [unprintable in *EIR*]," etc.... All were of course half naked and hip-hopping, giving the worst image of black Africans to an already disoriented population.

No wonder the children's concentration span is falling and, except for their attention to these voyeuristic shows, a majority of adults is no longer curious about how others live. This happens in our Europe where the social points of reference are collapsing, in a society controlled by those who pretend to fight for human rights. Europe has lost its positive sense because the ideals of social value are disappearing and there is no project for a better future. At best, people see the European Union and the euro as a protection against the others, a sort of giant condom, and certainly not as an Ode to Joy. See Macron pretending to love Europe and playing Beethoven's Ode to Joy like a mantra, while at the same time transforming the Elysée Palace into a giant and depraved night club.

Again, why am I nonetheless so sure that Europe is fit to join the New Paradigm? Because, as exemplified by Leibniz, Europe has within it the resources which can be revived and inspired. Europe and the United States have historically been the leaders of an active form of humanism.

It is Nicholas of Cusa, so dear to Helga Zepp-LaRouche, who explained how a human mind can create a higher order where all differences are transcended. In his late writings, he referred to it as the *posse facere omnia* or the *posse ipsum*, not knowledgeable by the human mind as a fixed point, but only through the becoming, the moment when human creativity meets the process of the universe, as when the light manifests itself in visible objects. It is in those moments that a human being is really, creatively human, contributing with new discoveries to the future of society, beyond the formal, established rules of logics, at a level where what was apparently contradictory is no longer so, that is, at a higher order. It is what Cusa called the "coincidence of the opposites," an inspiration to reach into the unknown future, something that the instructions of the European Union forbid.

The Best of Europe Instead

We can therefore say that as a construct, the European Union has raped the best of European culture, which our mission is to revive. The higher order in the macrocosm can only exist if there is the maximum possible development of all microcosms. Human beings should develop each in their maximum way and act in the interest of each other, and all nations should develop each in their maximum way and act in the interest of each other to have a harmonious world. It is the spirit of the Peace of Westphalia: To overcome war, you have to base your foreign policy on the curiosity for and the interest of the other.

It is the principle of a true Republic, and it is not only complementary but springs from the same cognitive and emotional source as *tianxia*. The principle is Humanity first, the aspiration for human beings and nations alike where, as Schiller said, duty and passion, necessity and freedom are one.

We have that in the storage drawers of our history. So let's stop our petty quarrels, let's stop behaving like children in a tragic playground and reread our philosophical classics to meet the ones of the East, and find our inspiration in Lyndon LaRouche's *Earth's Next Fifty Years*, written in 2004 but reaching through our future. I would also advise you to read Rabelais and Heine, especially Rabelais, to reject the unduly and criminal ruling powers with the weapon of creative laughter, against all careerists and courtesans regurgitating the answers and moods expected by the principalities and powers of a self-destructive world. Glass-Steagall, a National Bank, credit for infrastructure and development, fusion and the more advanced contributions of science: the four Laws of Lyndon LaRouche, not as proselytism to convert but as a common inspiration to build together.

Let me end, related to what I said, with a quote of Confucius: "If you meet a man of high value, try to be like him; if you meet a mediocre man, try to identify his shortcomings in yourself." This is one of the secrets to reach the *ren*—the sovereign good for the advantage of the other—in a harmonious world, to be the true citizen of a Republic or of a more perfect Union, not its caricature inhabited by self-satisfied nonentities. It is our instrument to reach into a future, to rediscover Europe as a pathway to the World Land-Bridge.

PROF. HANS KÖCHLER

The Re-Establishment of International Law

Hans Köchler, a retired Professor of Philosophy at the University of Innsbruck, Austria, is the founder and President of the International Progress Organization based in Vienna. This is an edited report, combining elements of his prepared address with the transcript of his speech. He spoke on Panel III of the Schiller Institute conference, on July 1, 2018.

Hans Köchler

Mr. Lyndon LaRouche, Mrs. Zepp-LaRouche, ladies and gentleman. As time is short, I will not read out the prepared text; I have forwarded it to the interpreters.

I will proceed in four steps to meet this challenging task that the organizers have given me, namely to say something about the *re-establishment* of international law.

The facts, of course, are clear and obvious; we see almost regularly that countries that are powerful, act as states—they regularly invade other countries, they destroy political system—"regime change" is now one of the buzzwords, and these nations are not held accountable. These countries are not held accountable, and the leaders who are responsible for the decisions are not held accountable.

For me, the most shocking example is what has happened since 2003: The United States has never met its responsibilities; has never had to shoulder its responsibility concerning the destruction of Iraq, and the leader at that time has never been brought to justice.

So, this is a very frustrating situation and it is obvious that there is *no* "international rule of law," in spite of the solemn commitment to this noble principle in the United Nations Charter.

So, now I will try to meet that challenge put before me, in four steps.

Diagnosis: Antagonism Between Law and Realpolitik

First, we have to be clear about what "law" is; unless we know what the nature of law is, we cannot make any assessment about re-establishing it.

The second question I will address here is: Do these criteria of law, the basic elements of law, really exist in the field of international law? Yes or no?

The third question will be, If—in what is called "international law"— the criteria of law are not met, what are the reasons for this state of affairs? Why is it so that in this now vast domain of rules and regulations—for which we use the notion of international law—there is not this nature of law? Why is it so that in fact, it is power that rules, but not law?

And, finally, the fourth point, if we have been able to identify the reasons, we may think about what to do about it; how to change that system; how to re-establish international law. But, this can only be undertaken if first we know what law is, and we know why things went wrong. Otherwise, we will only be led by illusions, and we will always have wrong expectations, and blame this United Nations organization for something it is not able to do, or maybe it was not even meant to do. We'll see.

Law is a system of norms, which is *enforced* by the state, according to a clear framework of regulations, and checks and balances. And, that is also what distinguishes a legal norm from a moral norm … If I violate a *legal* norm, there will be a consequence, there will be a sanction, and this can mean the removal of my freedom. Of course, I do not say that the legal norms are independent or the legal system is independent of morality; a legal norm has consequences in the real world, a moral norm (if I violate it) would have consequences in the metaphysical world. A system of law—this is my position—must be based on the common good, and must be based on human rights, or what others would call certain "natural" norms which cannot be changed.

So, if law is as I have now described it, the question is: Do we have law in this sense, in the international field? In the relations between states, is it so that if a state or a leader of a state violates norms of international law, there will be a sanction, and there will be action against the violator? Certainly not! This leads me to step two: We have enforcement of the law, at least on paper, namely in the United Nations Charter, and that is in just one particular field—that is about the use of force by one state against another state, including also the *threat* of the use of force.

UN Charter Specifies Impunity for Some

To serve justice, all law must be enforced consistently and comprehensively. If selective enforcement is the "modus operandi" of a legal system, it does not deserve to be called a system where the rule of law prevails. Because, in law there must be no double standards; there must be equality. So, that is exactly *not* the case in regard to international relations.

Let me explain why this is so in the third step. As I said, the UN Charter has this basic provision that the use of force, and the threat of the use of force, are illegal under international law. The issue is, there is a body with almost absolute powers in the United Nations—that is the Security Council. If it adopts decisions under the famous Chapter VII of the UN Charter—these are decisions on collective security (related to the enforcement of the ban on the use of force)—the first problem is, these decisions will only take effect if there is no veto cast by the five permanent members. The five countries have the privilege in a body that consist of 15 member states—they have the privilege to prevent any decision from being adopted (for which they are not obliged to give any reasons); it is their sovereign right. Of course, this is absolutely in total contradiction to one of the basic principles of the UN Charter, named right at the beginning of the Charter, namely, sovereign equality of states.

The big issue here is that those five states (that were the most powerful in 1945) themselves do not need to pay attention to the norm on the non-use of force, for they can prevent any decision for its implementation if it is against their interests.

The general norm that a party to a dispute shall abstain from voting—a common-sense principle of justice, so to speak—does *not* apply to decisions of the Council under Chapter VII. This means that a perma-

Xinhua/Li Muzi

United Nations Security Council meeting at the UN headquarters in New York, March 14, 2018.

nent member can commit an act of aggression against another state with full impunity. According to Chapter VII, the Council has the power, and can pass resolutions that all have legally binding effect on all member states of the United Nations, and these measures include the imposition of economic sanctions, diplomatic sanctions and also the use of military force—it's all at the discretion of the Council. If one is aware of the almost absolute power of the Council, it makes a mockery of justice.

Re-Establishment of International Law

This brings me to the last point: How to do something about this situation, or what could be done to re-establish international law. The UN, in its present form, lacks even basic procedural provisions for the enforcement of international law in a *consistent* manner.

Instead of linking permanent membership, connected with the veto privilege, to the power constellation of a bygone era, the Charter should redefine the notion of permanent membership—it should not be related to a single country, but to a region or regional organizations such as the African Union, Latin America, the European Union, the Association of South-East Asian Nations (ASEAN), etc. Any binding decisions under Chapter VII of the Charter would, thus, require consensus among all regions. This would be more democratic, a more responsible and acceptable use of the veto right, and would provide additional protection to smaller and weaker states against abuses of power by the organization's major players.

But, what also would be necessary is that, first and foremost, the wording of Chapter VII that somehow obliquely allows aggressor states to use the veto to protect themselves must be abolished. A legal ban on the use of force is simply not credible if an aggressor can be a judge in his own cause.

It would be so easy, in terms of drafting—it would just be necessary to eliminate a few words in paragraph 3 of Article 27.

There should be no illusion: Under present conditions, statutory as well as political, this is still a dream—because the holders of power and privilege will not easily agree to give up their dominant position However, the emerging *multipolar power constellation* may gradually convince those who have benefited the most from the status quo in the UN that continuing to insist on their privilege may ultimately be detrimental to the pursuit of their national interests (including their vital economic interests).

There is hope for the re-establishment of international law ... in view of the re-emergence of a new balance of power. We have seen the development of several regional groupings, such as the development of the BRICS grouping, and these new factors will become stronger in the near future.

That, in my view, means two things: First of all, the great powers that enjoy these privileges in the Charter will have to be more cautious in how they use this privilege. The other aspect is related to the large, global picture. Should the real international community at some point come to the conclusion that one cannot reform the Charter of the UN, the time may come that one has to think about a new beginning—and that means phasing out an organization that has been paralyzed, that cannot reform itself. Unconventional measures are possible; we have seen it also in the case of how the President of the United States acts, on issues that were considered almost intractable a short time ago. And as far as a world organization is concerned, it would be worth considering such a new statute, which would include the global regions as major players, and which would do justice to this principle of sovereign equality.

MARCO ZANNI

Has European Integration Gone Too Far?

Marco Zanni is a Member of the European Parliament, and is sitting within the Europe of Nations and Freedom (ENF) Group. He is also a member of the Lega Party, has professional experience in banking, and is therefore a member and representative of the EU Parliament's Committee on Monetary and Budgetary Affairs. He spoke on Panel III of the Schiller Institute conference, on July 1, 2018.

Good morning everyone! It's always a pleasure to address such an audience. It's the third time I have participated in a conference organized by the Schiller Institute, and it's a really nice experience.

Today, as Stefan said, I'm here to talk about the future of the European Union, and the question that I would like to pose today is a very important one. Last week on

Marco Zanni

Thursday and Friday, we had a European Council meeting which showed clearly that European countries are divided and are no longer able to make progress concerning the future of the European Union. There is no agreement on immigration, there is no agreement on the future of the Eurozone, and the only thing they have agreed upon is to keep to the status quo and kick the can down the street. That is becoming the main policy of the European Union. So, this question is very important to address, because people are getting angry with the failure of the European Union and the European institutions to solve the three main problems that they are facing today.

Europe's Failure to Solve Three Problems

First, the economic crisis is still ongoing in a lot of countries: Europe has one of the worst records of performance, in terms of economic growth, among the larger countries, or groups of countries, in the world. Second is the problem of internal security. People all over Europe are getting anxious about the lack of security we are experiencing in our cities all over Europe. The third big problem is the management of the flow of immigration into Europe. The impact of uncontrolled immigration into Europe has been very strong in the past years. The European Union has been largely ineffective in addressing this problem and in helping African and Middle Eastern countries in solving their problems. Europe has failed to improve conditions back home for those trying to reach the European Union, so that they would, instead, want stay in their home countries, having good opportunities there.

Addressing this, the European Union is sending a lot of money to those countries under what we call the Juncker Plan for Africa; it's a sort of financial engineering plan with a small amount of fresh money and a lot of financial engineering with fake money marketed around by the European Commission. On this point, the European Union should look at what the Chinese are doing in Africa and in other developing countries. Sending this money has been really ineffective for the European Union. We have not been able to create development in those countries. We have not created any value with the aid money that we sent to African countries.

The Chinese model, on the other hand, is very effective in its operation, because all the flow of money that the Chinese send to African countries, to Eastern Africa, to the Middle East, also to the Balkans, is strictly controlled by the Chinese government. And the results and the value that this money creates is strongly controlled by the government with a centralized strategy.

The European Union is delegating to private companies the management of the foreign aid to African countries, so we don't have control of the money that we send to Africa; we don't have the tools to control the effectiveness and the results in terms of growth, employment, and creating value for those countries using the money of European taxpayers. So, our policy in helping those countries is really ineffective. We should look at the Chinese model in order to eradicate the problem of immigration flows at the source.

On the economic crisis, it's pretty clear that the policies that the European institutions have pursued in the last seven years from the start of the Eurozone crisis in 2010, have been ineffective in restoring growth and employment in the Eurozone and in the whole European Union. Those mistakes created not only macroeconomic imbalances in the European Union, but they created strong divergence and balkanization of the European Union member states. What happened last week at the European Council—freezing all discussion about the future of the European Union, because there is no agreement and there is a lack of trust among the European countries, is a sign that we have to think about or rethink the cooperation among European countries.

It's pretty clear to everyone, not only in the European Union, but also outside the European Union—and I will talk later about the approach of the new U.S. administration toward Europe—it's pretty clear that Europe is divided. Europe cannot go on with forced integration that is being refused by the European people.

Has Integration Gone Too Far?

So, that's the main question of my speech: "Has integration gone too far?" And my reply and my thought about this question is "Yes". This forced integration is disintegrating Europe and European values, the European economy, and Europe as one of the most important contributors to the growth of the world economy and to civilization in the past centuries.

So, the big question that European leaders have to answer is, "Are we able to rethink and create a different institutional framework based on different values that could restore prosperity, cooperation, and solidarity in Europe?" That's the big question. It's clear that the actual institutional framework centralized in Brussels and in the European Union institutions—the commissions especially—is not succeeding in addressing the problems that European citizens have. It's clear that this fragmentation and the balkanization in the interests of the European Union are creating a huge problem for the stability, not only of countries that are still affected by the economic crisis, the so-called PIGS [Portugal, Italy, Greece and Spain], but of the whole European Union, including the countries that are considered positive examples and the winners in European integration.

The references to Germany are very strong; there is much talk about Germany vis-à-vis what is happening, and the lack of a sense of legitimacy of the European Union and the European Union institutions right now. The Chancellor of Germany has been, for years, the symbol of the unity and the values of the European Union, and has been seen as one of the stronger leaders in the European member states. The difficulties that the

Chancellor, Mrs. Merkel, is experiencing now, are the result of the wrong policies that she backed, and pursued, at the European Union level, not only on immigration—that probably today is the main issue debated in Germany—but also in fostering and feeding a wrong economic model on which the Eurozone is based.

This economic model is really fragile and is not sustainable. Why? Because it's too dependent on external factors. Our economy in the Eurozone is based on reducing internal costs—inflation and labor costs—to export our products outside the European Union, outside the Eurozone. So, we are supposed to pursue a larger external surplus in order to feed the economy at home. But this strategy is falling apart today because it is too dependent on the premise that external or third countries outside the Eurozone will absorb such a huge external surplus.

At the G-7 summit, European leaders Theresa May, Emmanuel Macron, and Angela Merkel face President Donald Trump (seated).

This is what is happening not only with the Trump administration, but with the United States. From the time of the Obama administration, the United States started to question the large external surpluses of the Eurozone and of Germany. So, the economic model on which the Eurozone is based, is too dependent on the decisions of third parties, of countries outside of the Eurozone. It's clearly not sustainable.

What about security? This is another very important problem that we are living with, in the European Union. Also, on this point, the European Union is too dependent on the decisions of third countries; NATO, the North Atlantic Alliance, is led by the United States in terms of investment in military capacity and in security. The European Union is not able, and has not been able, to build up a common military capacity, or to contribute its share to defense, to NATO. We are still too dependent on the United States for military defense—on a government that we do not control.

On the management of immigration flows, we are still too dependent on the decisions of, and the ability to make good agreements with countries in Africa and in the Middle East.

So, it's clear that the strategy the European leaders have pursued in the last seven years has been a total failure in addressing the three main issues, because we are too dependent on external decisions.

This situation should end very soon, because the political unsustainability of the framework on which the European Union is based, is totally wrong. We have to change the framework, and look instead for a form of cooperation—not just thinking about the composition of the European Union (the 27 member states that from March 2019 will be part of the European Union), but seriously considering the development of an alternative framework that could put the European Union on a positive track towards growth.

Europe as a Bridge

Regaining the geopolitical importance that Europe had in the past should include the role that the European Union and Europe as a bridge between the United States—the traditional international power that shaped all the international institutions in the 20th Century—and the rising power on the eastern side of the globe, China. Europe, if it returns to real economic growth, will regain a role as a connector between the new rising powers in the East and the new approach that the Trump administration has begun in international relations. Thanks to the approach that Mr. Trump took in recent G-7 meeting, with the new Italian Prime Minister [Giuseppe Conte], Italy has regained a geopolitical importance in the international debate.

Before the European Council meeting and other recent international meetings that the new Italian Prime Minister has participated in recently, many people said that due to the radical approach of the new Italian government, Italy would be isolated by the other countries. But the reality is that, thanks to the support of the United States, to the openness of the United States to the attempt to create a strong relationship also with China, and thanks to our Undersecretary of Economic Development, who has strong experience in China and in Chinese relations, Italy is regaining geopolitical importance in shaping the future of Europe.

A New Institutional Framework

We need, however, a new institutional framework that will shape a new era for Europe, a new era that is no longer based on centralization, on decisions taken by unelected bureaucrats in Brussels and by the European Central Bank. We need a new institutional framework that is respectful of the differences that the 27 member states of the European Union have. They are not only differences in the way in which we see and look at the economy and economic development; but they are also differences in political system, in the cultural systems that we have at the European Union level and in the member states.

So, the new institutional framework, if Europe is to survive this crisis, should be based on more subsidiarity. We should ask ourselves, "What is the common ground that we have today in the European Union and Europe? What are the common things that we can promote, for the common benefit and the mutual benefit of the European countries?" And on the other hand, "What are the topics on which the differences are too wide, in which the divergence is too big, and on which it is impossible to find common ground and agreement that can satisfy all the European countries?"

With more subsidiarity, while returning some competencies and powers to the national capitals, Europe can survive and can regain a path of growth and regain its role at the center of the geopolitical debate as a connector between the new U.S. approach to the international institutions and the rising powers in Asia and the Middle East. The work that the Italian government is trying to do in shaping this new institutional framework will be very important as an example to other European countries that want to pursue the same way.

Prospects After 2019

With this view in mind, what could happen after 2019? The year 2019 will be very important for the future of Europe and the European Union. In May we will have new elections for the European Parliament; so the European Parliament Assembly will be renewed. As you may know, the European Union institutions are mainly three: the European Council (the Council of the European Union); the Commission; and the Parliament.

We have member states, we have the Commission which should be a sort of executive, and we have the Parliament.

Today, the European Council has changed its view on the future of the European Union. With the Italian government, with the new Austrian government, with other governments with new parties joining the European Council, the approach on the future of the European Union will be more based on subsidiarity, on the defense of the interests of the European people, and on finding common ground on things that we can do better together. But after 2019, we will have another institution—the European Parliament—that will foster a change in European politics. We will probably have three big political families in the next European Parliament: From the one side, the traditional parties that are falling apart in terms of consensus and voters with a socialist orientation, will probably disappear. In the center, we will have this faker Macron who is supposed to be the new leader of European integration, the new leader who will bring Europe into a United States of Europe. Macron's power is falling apart in France; he is having grave difficulties domestically and he has no support in the Council for his proposal for reforming the European Union. On the other side, we will have a stronger group, even stronger than today, of the so-called euro-critics who will shape strongly the politics of the European Parliament.

If Europe wants to be saved, then we have to change radically our institutional framework, with no more centralization in Brussels, with no more decisions and economic systems focussed on the needs of the big banks and the City of London, but a cooperative system that is respectful of the differences of the national states, of the spaces of democracies, and of the decisions and willingness of the European people. Europeans don't want to have a United States of Europe. They just want to have equal cooperation among European nations and sovereign states, in order to bring more prosperity to Europe and the world, and to solve the three main problems that they are experiencing today that I mentioned earlier in my speech.

Conclusion

My hope is that in the near future, other governments will join the new Italian government in this effort to reform Europe with more equal, stable, and solid institutions. Without this reform that we strongly need, the European Union is condemned to failing and creating a huge geopolitical crisis at the heart of the world.

Let me conclude by saying that our Europe will reform in that sense, or the European Union will be finished and European countries will be affected by a new crisis that will be stronger than the one that we experienced after 2010. Our system is dysfunctional; our system is unequal and is fostering divergences and imbalances inside Europe. We have to change it. My hope is that we will be able to change it very quickly. If not, the European Union will finish very soon in a disorganized way, creating huge suffering for the European people. But I am confident that new politicians and new parties rising all around Europe will be able to change it as soon as possible.

Thank you very much.

DR. ARMIN AZIMA

The Controllable Energy

Armin Azima

Dr. Armin Azima is a staff scientist at the University of Hamburg. This is an edited report, combining elements of his power points with the transcript of his speech. He spoke on Panel III of the Schiller Institute conference, on July 1, 2018.

Ladies and Gentleman, dear conference board, and dear Helga Zepp-LaRouche. Thank you very much for the invitation to give this talk. It is an honor for me to be here and I believe that I will convince the audience that physics in our modern world is very exciting. Promising developments are currently ongoing, about which you maybe even haven't heard so far. Thus, please allow me to inform you and simultaneously entertain you with the marvelous progress in the field of energy technology, which we can witness today in the world.

In this talk I will concentrate on the following topics: I will provide you with some interesting numbers on the progress of German energy transition and what it means practically for the German people. Then I will focus on two hot spots of nuclear science in the world, which are very promising and provide the hope of having a very nice future with cheap, clean and powerful energy sources. Especially the mastering of fusion technology will open the gate to a new, wonderful world with possibilities that are currently unthinkable. And I would like to present you some ideas of what could be done, if power were cheap. However, in the history of mankind, we all know that every technology can be used for the sake of prosperity or for destruction. And of course the stronger and more powerful the technology, starting from the invention of steel, up to the first fission of an atomic nucleus, the higher the hazard of the correlated weapon. That's why I feel it to be my responsibility to speak out loudly against the deployment and use of nuclear weapons in general here, which I will underline scientifically in the last section of my talk.

LaRouche's Four Laws

Before I discuss technology, however, I would like to mention LaRouche's Four Laws, the First of which is the reconstitution of the Glass-Steagall Act, and the

Second being the introduction of a national banking system.

LaRouche's Third Law concerns the continuous increase of the general energy flux-density of society in general. This demand includes the further development of civil infrastructure to be able to make use of powerful energy sources for increases in the productive physical economic output.

LaRouche's Fourth Law, a topic that is important for me personally, being a physicist, is the research for the development of the utilization of nuclear fusion as an energy source, which in my personal belief provides the only possibility of maintaining a high level of prosperity in a growing world, for all mankind into the future.

But let me at first start with one of the major aspects in LaRouche's Four Laws, and that is the energy flux-density.

Consequences of Germany's Energy Transition

As a consequence of the well-known transition to regenerative energy sources in Germany I have created a map of all of the installed wind turbines in Germany, which are plotted as brown spots. Together, in 2016, they generate about the same amount of power as the seven red spots representing the nuclear power plants. And as you may know, those red spots will all disappear by 2022, when Germany's national exit from nuclear power generation will be fulfilled. The wide spread of power generators, which we in Germany call "decentralization of energy production," requires a complex and expensive power transport network—especially as compared to the time when the power mix was dominated by a few powerful central power plants about 20 years ago.

Energy costs have risen, and will rise still further in the future. Currently, we have fulfilled a transition to about 30% of

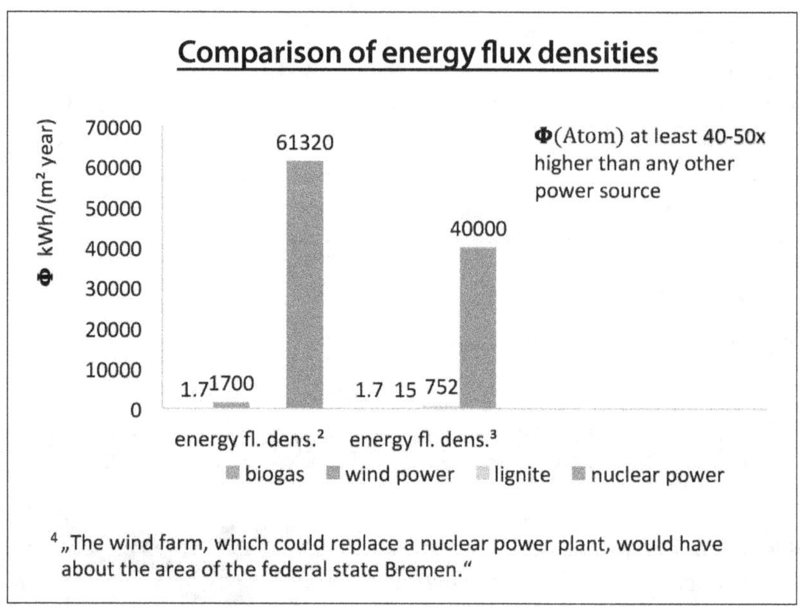

The energy flux-density (Φ) of nuclear power vastly exceeds that of other power sources, for example, biogas, wind, and brown coal. Shown here are two sets of calculations of Φ. The author's calculations are the bars on the left and those of Dr. Günter Keil, on the right. (Some bars are too small to be visible.) The quotation is from the news program Tagesschau.

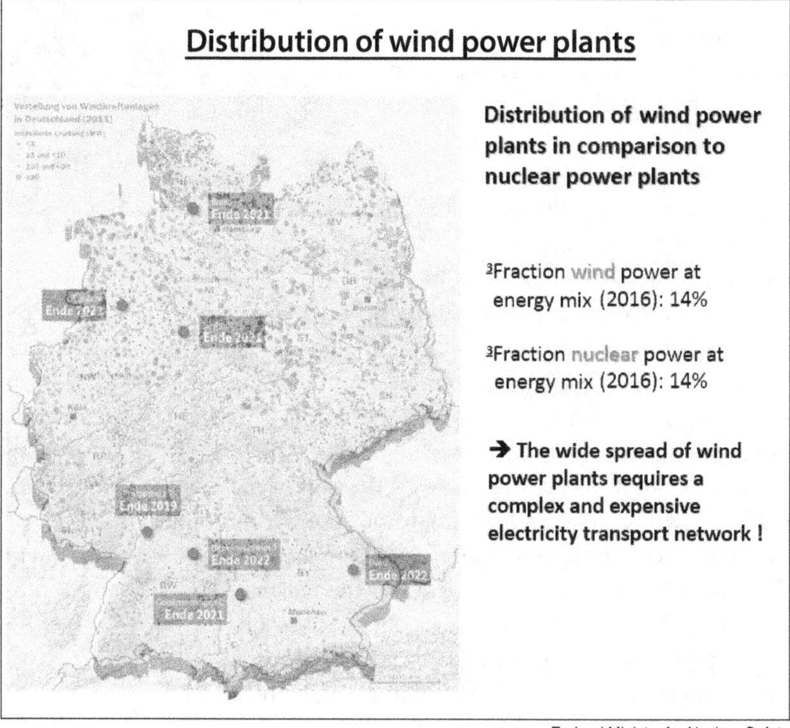

Federal Ministry for Nuclear Safety

Germany is covered with wind farms (brown spots), all of which, in 2016, produced as much power as the seven nuclear power plants (red spots). But the red spots are to disappear by 2022, when Germany is to completely exit from nuclear power. The key, upper left, shows installed capacity of wind farms in megawatts by size and color of the spots, as of 2011.

regenerative energy sources in our energy mix and the electricity price has increased by more than 50%, inflation-adjusted. And the goal is to reach 80% in the year 2050! The federal government however, claims that electricity prices will decrease again after 2025, to which I would add the word "maybe." We will see.

I have calculated the final power bill for Germany and compared it to France, which has more than 50% of nuclear generated power in its electricity mix. Sure, Germany is a wealthy country and many people can afford the higher energy prices, not all, but many. Even for a comparably large and comparably densely populated developing country, a power bill of 150 billion euro per year would be definitely too high. Hence, the French energy mix might be better suited to their needs, to say it in diplomatic words.

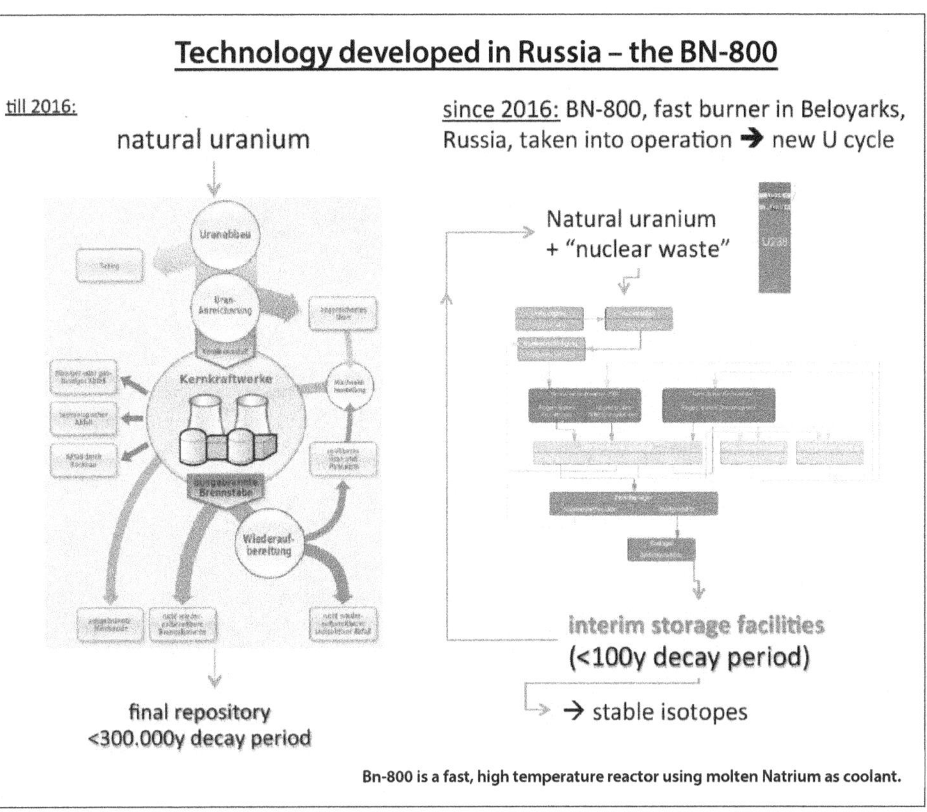

Nuclear Power as Such

Let's now concentrate on nuclear power in detail. As we have learned, the energy flux-density of nuclear fission power is currently the highest technologically

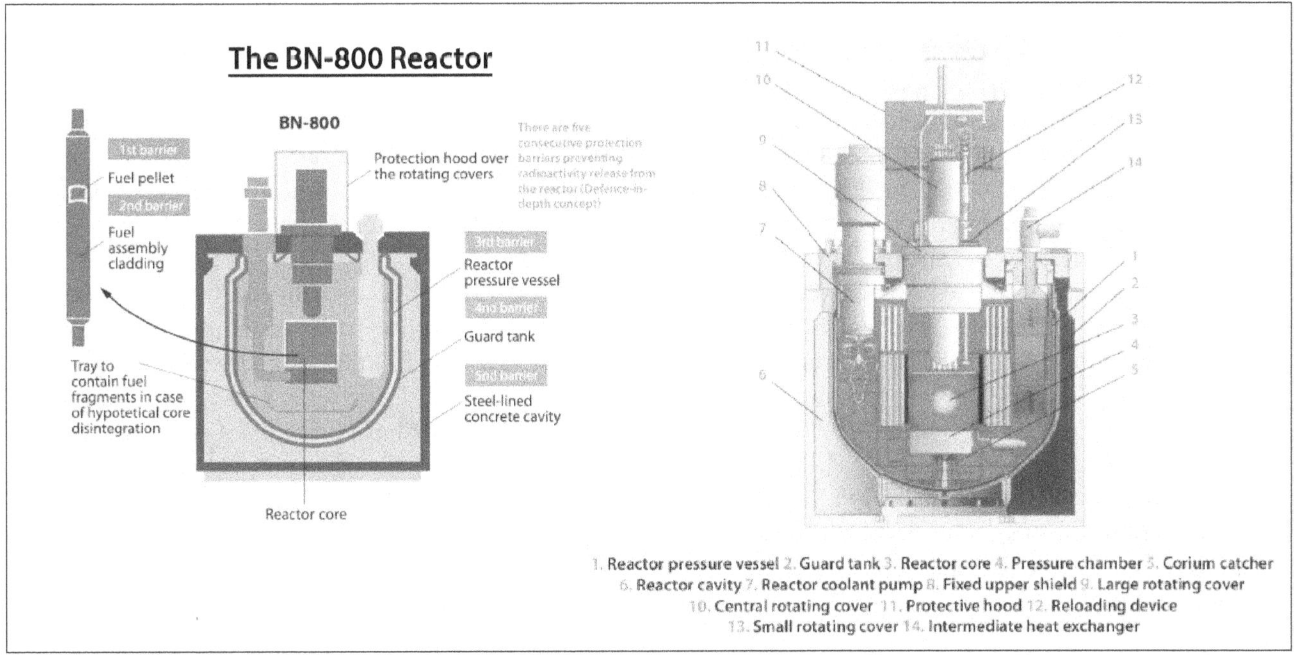

available of all power sources today.

Despite that fact, the German federal government has decided to fully exit nuclear power technology in Germany by the year 2022. The question is, "Why?" From a rational standpoint there can only be the following three criticisms, three reasons: the problem of nuclear waste disposal, reactor safety, and the prevention of proliferation of nuclear weapons. Due to limited time I will concentrate on the first point.

First some fast basics. Our general nuclear reactors are light-water reactors,

*Two plasma rings are collided with $250\,km/s$ and form a toroidal plasma (FRC[3]) in the collision, which stabilizes itself **without outer** compressing magnetic field.*

which work with thermal, hence "slow" neutrons. The chain reaction is then greatly improved, since the slow neutrons interact with the fuel much more efficiently. However, this has a price: the neutrons lose the ability to crack isotopes of even mass number, which significantly decreases the amount of possible fuel materials for these reactors.

Natural uranium consists mainly of the isotope U-238, with an even mass number, which cannot be fissioned by the thermal, slow neutrons. Hence U-238 is artificially enriched by the isotope U-235. After three years of operation, most of the U-235 is burned up, while the amount of U-238 is almost the same as at the beginning. But new materials have been created in the process, such as plutonium and other minor actinides, which we refer to as "nuclear waste."

Natural uranium becomes enriched, and then burned. The waste is separated and finally disposed of, and part of the fuel rod is recycled and reused in this process. The problem: The final repository must safely contain the waste.

The Russian 'Fast Burner,' BN-800

Russia has chosen another way. Since 2016, a new reactor type, called BN-800 has been brought on line. This reactor is called a "fast burner," not to be confused with a "fast breeder." The BN-800 is not a breeder reac-

tor, it's a burner. It uses "fast" neutrons, and thus their neutrons can, with similar efficiency, fission *all* the heavy isotopes including those with even mass number! And that's the trick; this reactor is now capable of reusing its "waste" as new fuel in a long cycle, over and over again. The much smaller fraction of nuclear "waste" compared to conventional reactors, has an additional advantage, in that it decays way faster. After only 100 years, this "waste" can be taken out of storage. Thus, with this technology, a *final* disposal repository is no longer needed!

To make it perfectly clear, the BN-800 can burn "nuclear waste" as if it were conventional nuclear fuel. No final depository is needed for the end-products of this reactor. And this reactor is in operation *now* at this very moment!

The BN-800 has de-defined the word "nuclear waste," because what is the waste now? Actually, it is exactly as Lyndon LaRouche predicted about ten years ago, when he said, "There exists no nuclear waste, only we currently do not have the technology to make use of the end products."

So, I delete this bullet point from the list of criticisms of nuclear power. Problem solved! Let's quickly move to another topic. I would like to show you some recent news concerning fusion research.

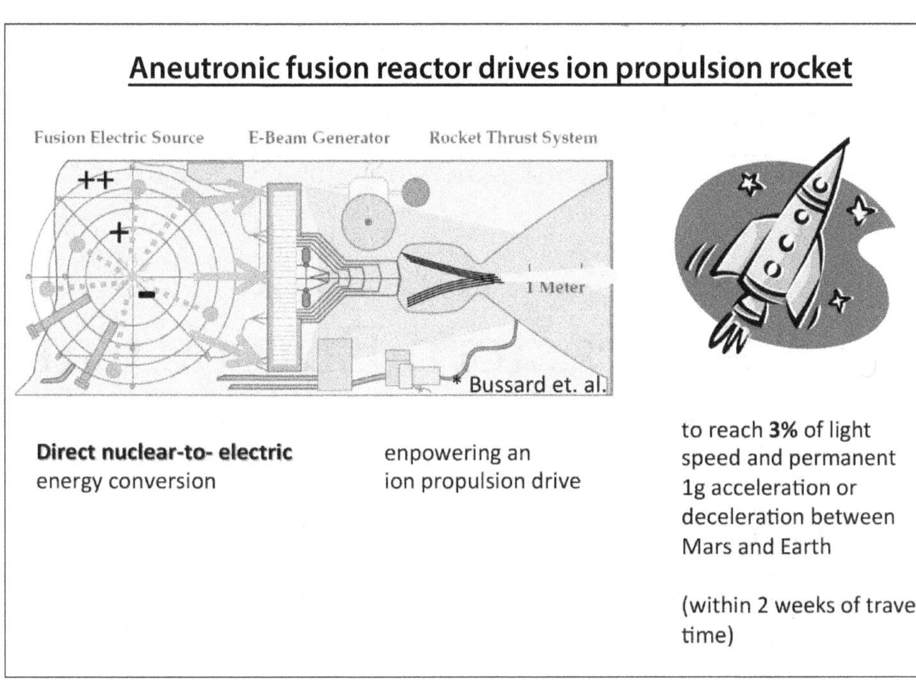

Direct nuclear-to- electric energy conversion

enpowering an ion propulsion drive

to reach **3%** of light speed and permanent 1g acceleration or deceleration between Mars and Earth

(within 2 weeks of travel time)

Aneutronic Fusion

I would like to introduce to you a company called Tri-Alpha Energy from California. The mission of this company is to master a special form of nuclear fusion, which is vastly unknown, that is the p-B-11 reaction [the fusion of a proton with a boron-11 nucleus]. The special feature here is the aneutronic character of the end products. Classical fusion devices, such as the ITER tokamak project, are built to use D-T (deuterium-tritium) fuel, which mainly burns to neutrons as end product. But those little fellows are hard to make use of as they are electrically neutral and permeate matter easily, and thus cannot be easily transferred to electricity.

Two rings of plasma collide in the center. At the collision point, the two rings merge and form a donut shaped plasma sphere, which can stabilize and contain itself. The longest this machine has been able to keep the plasma stable, is more than 10 milliseconds. Recently they have also shown that they can reach high temperatures of up to 20 million degrees Celsius, which are milestones for this project.

Of course there is still a long way to go to reach finally 3 billion degrees Celsius for one second. But because the end products are positively charged, the direct conversion of the fusion energy to electricity works with 90% efficiency—no steam production, no turbine, is needed, which greatly reduces the size, and makes possible a 100 megawatt reactor of the size of a truck!

We can dream about future machines, as for example, what the U.S. physicist Robert Bussard has proposed. The direct nuclear-to-electricity conversion would allow us to empower an ion propulsion engine to continuously accelerate (or decelerate) a rocket at a rate equivalent to ± 1g up to a few percentage points shy of the speed of light speed. This would reduce the travel time between Earth and Mars to less than about two weeks! All the inner planets would become reachable. Yes, of course, at the moment it sounds like a dream, but scientists are really working on these kinds of engines.

What If …

And this brings me directly to more visions, of what would be possible with such a fusion reactor. What if power were extremely cheap and what if energy were available in abundance? We could think of desalination of seawater on a large scale or artificial petroleum synthesis, or, one of my favorite ideas, which is a revolutionary waste recycling system, which not only burns waste to CO_2 and ashes, but uses even more power to transform the ashes into a plasma state. Of course, this is a very energy-consuming process, using the arc-plasma technology. But in the plasma state we would be able to crack down any component, any material, in to its molecules or even atoms, which plasma could then be further re-sorted and extracted element-wise out of the "waste"—an almost perfect ~ 100% recycling. We finally arrive at an end of hunger and thirst for all of us!

Last but not least, please let me remind you again about LaRouche's last two Laws. Keeping in mind what I presented before, I think these demands are neither abstract nor unrealistic. Instead, reaching these goals would make our world better in all aspects, and that is why we should keep on working to realize them.

Thank you for your attention.

ELKE FIMMEN

How Eastern & Southeastern Europe Can Join in Making a Global Economic Miracle

Elke Fimmen of the Schiller Institute (Germany) spoke on Panel IV of the Schiller Institute conference, on July 1, 2018.

It is obvious, that the so-called leading nations of Western Europe finally have to do their homework and realize that only by cooperating with China's Silk Road Project, with Russia, and with the Eurasian Economic Union, can long-term prosperity, stability and peace, as we have discussed at this conference, be achieved. Peace through development is the North Star to follow—

Elke Fimmen

otherwise, with the old methods, Europe will blow up—and that cannot be an option.

To even propose to still extremely poor nations such as Albania and Macedonia that they set up refugee centers in exchange for EU-membership, is no policy but just mindless—and dangerous—lunacy.

Do we really want to again destabilize the still-fragile Balkan countries, after what they went through with the geopolitically motivated wars and the so-called "transformation" in the 1990s and 2000s, by insisting on old geopolitical power games and denying these nations their long-overdue economic development?

Is it not much more preferable to instead support plans such as that of Albanian President Edi Rama, who has drafted a 15-year plan for national development, including modernizing infrastructure and connecting with China's new Silk Road? And why would the EU oppose and put pressure against the project to build the long-overdue Peljesac Bridge in Croatia? Or against the construction of the Belgrade-Budapest high-speed railway, as a crucial component in the connection of Piraeus port in Greece through Macedonia, Serbia and Hungary with Central and Western Europe?

Will this EU-blockade and the insistence on austerity policies, such as not accepting Chinese loans for projects, contribute in *any way* to overcoming the wounds of the past and create a common future perspective for all of the populations of these countries?

Albanians still remember with horror—and we should as well—the desperation and chaos of the 1990s, when after the collapse of the communist system, 25,000 Albanians fled to Italy on boats; then after 5 years of so-called "western market reforms," the horrendous speculative pyramid-scheme collapsed, which cost most of the population its miniscule savings, and which led to countrywide breakdown of the social and state order, plundering by desperate people, and the deaths of more than one thousand. Finally the Organization for Security and Cooperation in Europe intervened and international peace troops from Greece, Italy, Spain, France, Turkey and Romania restored order and the basic functions of the state. In 1999, 300,000 Kosovarians fled to Albania, a country of 2.8 million with an average age of about 33 years, which posed again huge challenges to that country.

Now there is talk about a new "Albanian" Balkan route for refugees, because many refugees try to come from Greece via Albania, Montenegro, Bosnia, and then through Croatia and Slovenia, to Western Europe. Many already in Serbia—where the borders are closed to Hungary and Croatia—are now entering Bosnia, which has a 1,000 km border with Croatia. This creates new tensions among these neighboring countries, including a new crisis coming up in Bosnia. No new camps anywhere will stop this dynamic, only real global economic development can!

In this situation, the upcoming 16+1 Central and Eastern European leaders' meeting in Sofia, Bulgaria next weekend, which will be addressed by Chinese Prime Minister Li Keqiang, provides an excellent opportunity for Western European nations to team up and support the initiatives for growth and progress, which will be discussed there, instead of continuing to stall and blackmail nations for cooperating with China.

China's successful policy reflects proven principles of economic science, which have long been neglected in the West, despite the fact that these same methods were essential for the establishment of the USA, Germany, France, Japan, and others nations, as industrial nations.

Physical economics prioritizes the *planting of productive powers of nations*, as German-American economist Friedrich List called it, as opposed to the British Empire's global financial looting and so-called "free trade."

On the contrary, in physical economy, large infrastructure projects and a focus on science and technology are key for increasing the productivity of nations. The true wealth of nations is indeed the development of the *creativity of its population.*

China's New Silk Road, or BRI, is generating a whole new Eurasian network of cross-continent infrastructure and trade ties. It has also opened up the long-overdue opportunity for Central, Eastern and South Eastern European countries, to re-industrialize their national economies and to fulfill their productive potential, in agriculture, machine-building, high technology and research (e.g., in the nuclear sector) and to finally overcome the disastrous effects of neoliberal "shock therapy" and the social and economic destruction wrought by the geopolitically instigated series of Balkan wars of the 1990s.

Docking the Belt and Road with Europe

After the crash of 2007/2008, many Eastern European countries looked for new strategic opportunities to restart their economies. While the EU imposed vicious austerity and only saved the bankrupt banks, China initiated the format 16+1 with Central and Eastern European

Xinhua/Szilard Voros

Defense officials of six Central European nations and Poland, agreed to better protect the borders of Schengen zone, Budapest, March 28, 2018.

Countries (CEECs) and started annual leaders' meetings, the first one in Warsaw, Poland (2012), with the next one to take place this coming weekend in Sofia, Bulgaria.

The 16 CEE countries, diverse as they are, are a crucial bridge, due to their geographical location, for making the infrastructural and economic development of Eurasia through the New Silk Road/BRI infrastructure projects work. They span Europe from north to south, between the huge Russian market and Western Europe.

In his speech at the last 16+1 Leaders' Summit in November 2017 in Budapest, Chinese Premier Li Kexiang spoke about presenting "a new blueprint for the future." He presented an ambitious program for increased China-CEEC cooperation by "docking" the Belt and Road Initiative with the development strategies of the CEECs. China, he said, is aiming for a "prospering Europe." Closer ties with the 16 countries, which include 11 European Union members, would "usefully complement" EU-China relations.

He pointed out, that the 19th Party Congress developed new guidelines and perspectives for a more open and prosperous China, thus opening more and greater opportunities to all countries in the world. The Prime Minister estimated China's imports over the next five years should total $8 trillion, as it has moved from a phase of high-speed growth to high-quality growth.

Besides calling for accelerating key connectivity projects such as the Hungary-Serbia high-speed railway, Prime Minister Li proposed expansion of production capacity building, through economic and trade cooperation zones and by creating an industrial, value and logistics chain. He also called for the promotion of cooperation between small and medium-sized enterprises (SMEs), a subject extremely important for all CEE nations, which urgently want to develop their own high-technology industry *Mittelstand* and other productive facilities.

This approach of facilitating real growth and development through infrastructural, scientific and other productive investments, has created a new optimistic impetus in Eastern Europe and the Balkan countries, which is long overdue.

While European transport corridors were defined by the 1994 European Transport Ministers Crete conference, these projects did not get off the ground or only to an insignificant degree. Only with EU-expansion of Eastern countries after 2004, did things slowly start to move. But even today, the trans-European transport network can be best described as patchwork, with present EU-funding not providing for an integrated, high-priority approach. While real needs to bring the existing Trans-European Transport Network up to speed are today in the range of a minimum 500 billion euros between 2021 and 2030, as demanded in the recent Ljubljana Declaration by transport and related sector representatives, the budget now for the Connecting Europe Facility for Transport subsidy program will be only 30.5 billion euro. The budget for 2014-2020 is even less, at 21.3 billion euro.

On the contrary, in CEEC-China cooperation, transnational and Eurasian transport and logistics are a key feature. In May 2016, the 16+1 Secretariat for Logistical Cooperation was inaugurated in Riga, the capital of the Baltic state of Latvia; and in October 2017, the Warsaw Secretariat for Maritime Cooperation was opened. The "Riga Declaration" identifies "Adriatic-Baltic-Black Sea Seaport Cooperation" as a central issue, which should focus on the development of—

> … transportation hubs involving ports and industrial parks in the coastal areas of the Adriatic, Baltic and Black Sea and along the inland waterways, working together to build industrial clusters in ports and establishing modern road, rail and river corridors to connect them. …"

This would serve ".. the development needs of all 17 countries, and would thereby contribute to closer EU-China relations, by synergizing their specific demands and advantages for infrastructure development and industrial upgrad-

Xinhua

Chinese Premier Li Keqiang speaks to the Meeting of Heads of Government of Central and Eastern European Countries and China, in Riga, Latvia, Nov 5, 2016.

ing,… with a view to facilitating economic growth of each country and across the region …

China will provide another $1 billion for the second phase of capitalization of the China-Central and Eastern Europe Investment Cooperation Fund. The fund plans to invest 10 billion euro in the CEEC-region. Poland and Hungary are full members of the Asian Infrastructure Investment Bank, and Romania was accepted as a prospective member in May 2017.

These are just a few examples of such cooperation and its potential—about which you can read much more in the Schiller Institute's just published work, *The New Silk Road Becomes the World Land-Bridge, Volume II*, on the progress of the World Land-Bridge.

Conclusion

With the global shift toward a new paradigm of "peace through economic development," which we have been discussing during this conference, Central, Eastern and Southeastern European nations finally will be able to concentrate on the real development of their nations, instead of being abused as a geostrategic "cordon sanitaire" or military staging areas against Russia. China's initiative for the New Silk Road has created, along with Russia and the Eurasian Economic Union, the potential for a durable peace strategy for all of Europe, Eurasia, Africa and beyond. This second chance after 1989, cannot and must not be missed by the European nations.

Let us now create a true humanist renaissance in Europe, for the benefit of the world and mankind. Thank you!

The New Paradigm from the View of the Balkans

Professor Dr. Ivo Christov is a Member of the Bulgarian Parliament. He spoke on Panel IV of the Schiller Institute Conference, on July 1, 2018.

Thank you very much! Let me begin by thanking the Schiller Institute for inviting me to be here and to share some ideas and thoughts concerning this topic of our conference. I think that it will be a fruitful conference, not only in ideas, but also in practical activities.

The topic of my presentation today is "The New Paradigm from the View of the Balkans." As a scholar, I want to start from a top-down strategy, especially from the whole picture of the geopolitical present now, to our topic the Balkans and the new Chinese initiatives. There is the saying attributed to Napoleon, shared by the famous French historian, Fernand Braudel, that "geography is destiny."

World Power Centers

If we look at a geographical map, and look at the main industrial, economic power centers in the world now, we get an important perspective. From an historical standpoint, the first industrial circle is the Western center of the power—economic, military, and so on. It's situated in the south of Britain in England, and after that in the Ruhr region in the western part of Germany and the northeast part of France. It's a process that has been continuous for 200 years in the era of the so-called Industrial Revolution.

The result of this is that western countries, especially Great Britain, and after that of course France, and after that Germany and the United States, have very strong power not only in terms of their militaries, but in terms of their economies and especially in their cultural

Ivo Christov

views. It's very obvious that this is a western-centered world, because the center of power—especially military, economic, and technological— is concentrated here. Their predominance obviously derives from their military forces, their military power, by sea especially.

After that, at the very end of the Industrial Revolution, the next center of political and military power is North America, concentrated especially in the eastern part of the United States—the New England region. And after that, the center moved slowly, after the American Civil War, to the very center of the Great Plains in Chicago, and after that to the West Coast of the United States today. That transformed a very powerful center of military might and economy; it's the strongest center, because it is obvious that Canada and Mexico are countries which are very dependent on the American power. Between the Western European center and the American center, there are very intensive flows of goods, finance and so on.

After the Second World War, America became the major player in this game. Western Europe, and after 1989 Eastern Europe, became dependent on American power. Another center of economy and military power, is of course Russian. The Russians came into power after the reforms of Peter the Great, and especially after the establishment of the Soviet Union. During the Stalin period, the Soviet Union became the strongest power in the world in the military fields after the United States.

The fourth center of power—economic, military, trade, and so on—is the eastern part of Eurasia. First of all, historically, has been Japan, and after that Korea, and China.

What is typical for this center of economic and cul-

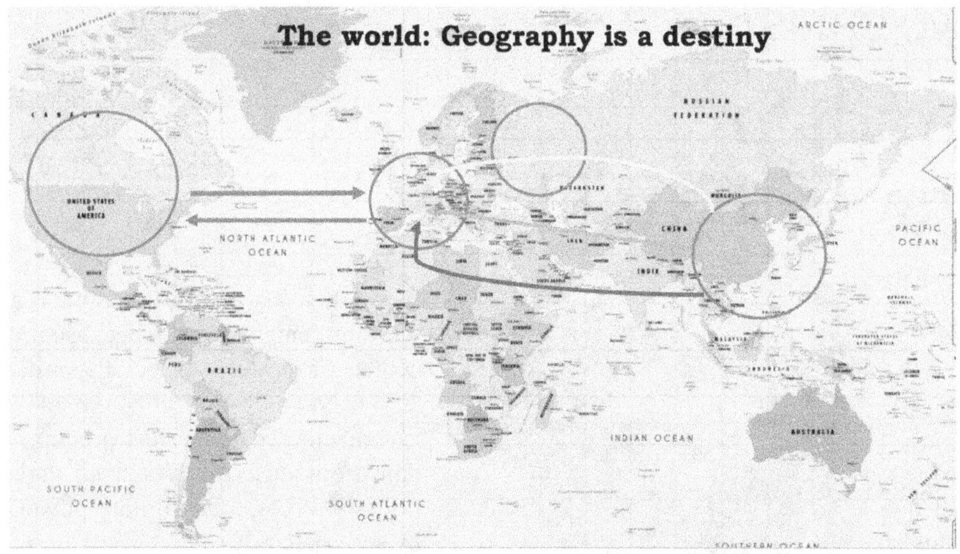

countries for energy resources.

So, what is principally new in our situation now? The principal situation is that China wants to develop its own activities and its own political and economic role in the world—not engaging in a zero-sum strategy, but from a strategy of win-win: "We win and you win in our collaborations and trade and political relationships." The dependency of China on resources, especially from this region, is an advantage for China, but there are some opportunities, especially from the North American countries, to block and stop China's development into becoming the leadership in the modern world.

tural influences? This is a very specific model of the establishment of modern culture, especially in the modern state of economy. This economy was created top down by the state, by a very strong state. This is nothing like the free market; all of its economy is a fruit of active state policy. It's typical for Japan at the beginning of the 20th Century. After that, during the reforms in China, after the 1980s, it is seen in China. This is a very specific collaboration between a strong state, on the one hand, and the creation of new economic fields and agents, on the other. In China's case, China's state creates the new economic champions on the market level in the world plain.

The Pursuit of Trade and Resources

Between the Western European core of Western power and the North American core of Western power, there is very intensive development of trade and other economic activities. What is very interesting is that their economic and political power is based on resources. Especially oil and gas resources, which are situated outside these regions with the exception of Russia. For example, for America, this is the oil and gas resources in the Mexican Gulf and Mexico, and of course in Canada and Alaska. On the other hand, in Europe, countries get their resources especially from the Gulf States in the Middle East, North Africa, and Africa as a whole. It is very interesting that for the Far East region economic model, it's very important to have a very strong linkage with the Middle Eastern countries and North African

Maritime Chokepoints

How? Because America for now controls, for example, the very important point, the Strait of Malacca, for example. The Strait of Malacca is absolutely important because through it goes 40% of world trade and exchange of goods, especially trade from China, from Japan, from Korea, from other so-called Asian tigers.

Another point for stopping China, is the Strait of Hormuz, between Iran and Oman, because this is the focal point for reaching the oil fields of the Middle East.

Another chokepoint, is the strait between the Arabian Peninsula and Africa, between Yemen and Djibouti—it is very interesting in regard to the lecture yesterday about this topic—and Djibouti, Somalia, and Ethiopia. Shipping between the Indian Ocean and the Mediterranean Sea must pass through Bab-el-Mandeb and the Suez Canal. In this point of view, it's very interesting to see China's strategy of developing new belts of international trade and cooperation, not only via oceans, but inland inside of Eurasia, especially from the western part of China via central Asia, Iran, and after that Turkey, to the center of Europe.

Europe, especially Germany, France, and the core

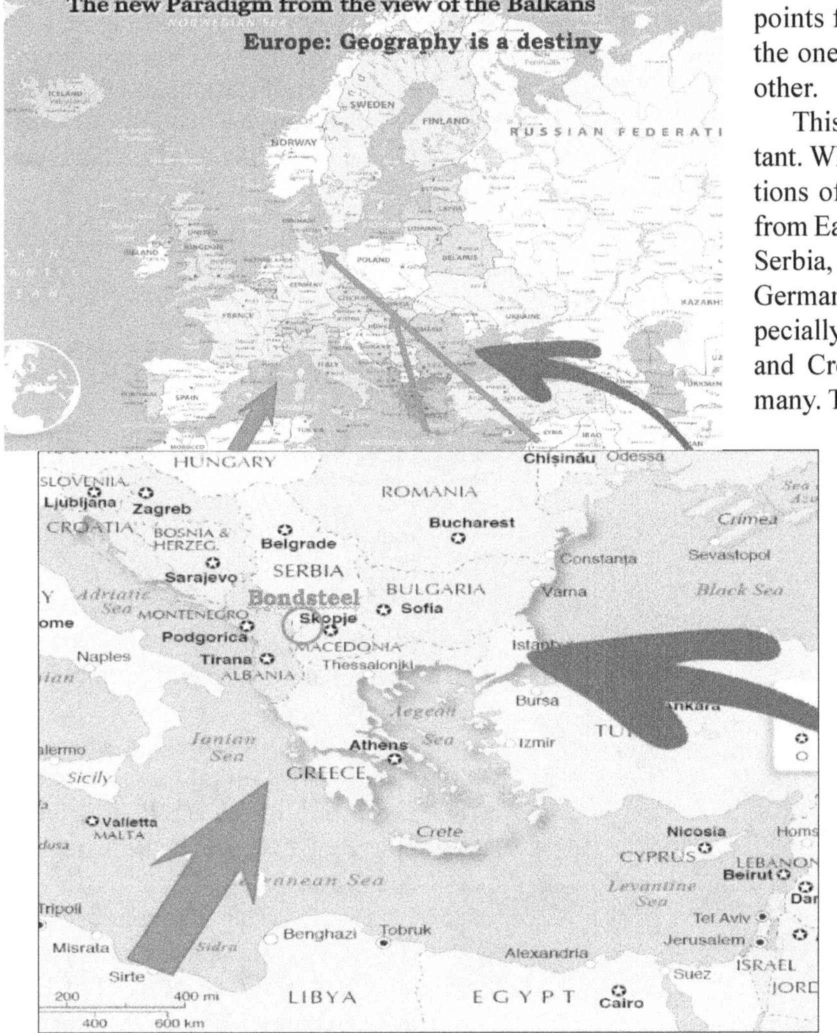

sula and the Balkan Peninsula are the two points for entering into Europe from Africa on the one side, and from the Middle East on the other.

This specific region is therefore very important. Why? First of all, there are two main directions of trade—goods and people and so on—from East to West via Turkey, Istanbul, Bulgaria, Serbia, and others to Central Europe; especially Germany. Another road is from North Africa, especially Egypt, via Greece, Macedonia, Serbia, and Croatia or Hungary directly also to Germany. This is very important for the blockage of these trade flows from the Balkans to Central Europe. Another important thing is that here, in this small peninsula, there is so much history, so many contradictions, and so many histories of bloody conflict. Why? Here, three civilizations live together—Muslims especially. This is part of the past history of the Ottoman Empire—Turks or Muslims in Bosnia or Albania. Another is the Orthodox civilization—the Greeks, Bulgarians, Serbians and Romanians are Orthodox. And of course, there is the Catholic civilization—concentrated in the northwest of the peninsula, especially in Croatia, the Croatian parts of Bosnia, and Slovenia. So, in this very small part of Europe is the battlefield of four major powers: the United States, Russia, Turkey, and China.

Will the Roads Be Open or Blocked?

What's interesting for China? China wants to enter into this very important area. China, in cooperation with Turkey, for example, completed a railway from Turkey via Istanbul and maybe to Bulgaria—but maybe only. Another railway project is from the Greek port of Piraeus directly to Thessaloniki, Macedonia, Serbia, and going to the very center of Germany. Let us talk about Bondsteel. It is the biggest American military camp in Europe, situated in Kosovo. From here, the United States has blocked every effort to enter into the Balkan Peninsula from any direction.

In the future, the project of the New Silk Road will be very difficult in practice. Why? There are so many

of Europe, is the biggest market now in the world. On the other hand, there is another option from Beijing via the southern part of Russia or the northern part of Kazakhstan directly to the Baltic ports and Germany. Another option is the southern route, from southern China via Thailand; or another option is from western China directly via Pakistan to the Pakistani Baluchistan province; this provides a direct linkage to the oil fields of the Middle East and the Gulf.

Many Roads Lead Through the Balkans

So, what is important here? Why do I speak about this if my topic is the Balkans? It's very interesting in historical, military, economic, and other dimensions to understand the situation here. Why are the Balkans so important? Not because I am from this region; I am from Kiev and I live in Bulgaria. The Iberian Penin-

obstacles, especially from the American strategy to stop China from engaging here, and to stop any activities in oil or gas initiatives by Russia to build new pipelines from Russia, via Bulgaria for example, to Serbia and Central Europe.

What should we do? Why is it so important for Europe to change the geopolitics in this region? If the Balkans remain nothing but a black hole to Europe, this geopolitics will interfere, if not stop, all the initiatives for entering and changing the geopolitical situation not only in Europe, but in the world. Thank you very much.

FOLKER HELLMEYER

Options for Integration of the Eurasian Economic Union and China's OBOR

Folker Hellmeyer is a German economist. This is an edited report based on his prepared text. He spoke on Panel IV of the Schiller Institute conference, on July 1, 2018.

The tremendous rise of Asian nations, which we have experienced for decades, is unparalleled in economic history. It's not just about China or India. The entire continent no longer accepts the supremacy of the old industrial nations. While our western world is struggling with aging, political fatigue, and debt, most Asian countries are characterized by growth and a young population capable of learning, which perseveres and is efficient. The emancipation of the emerging countries is reflected in the setting up of their own structures, be it the Asian Infrastructure Investment Bank as an alternative to the World Bank, or the New Development Bank as an alternative to the IMF, or CIPS [the Cross-Border Interbank Payment System] as a counterpart to SWIFT. The One Belt One Road (OBOR) project is the response of emerging countries to the disregard for their interests and to the shift in the financial economic power axis in favor of the emerging countries, whose share has risen from around 20% of world GDP to more than 66%.

Consequences

1. The massive shift of the financial-economic power axis renders a shift in the political power axis

Folker Hellmeyer

inevitable. The path leads from unilateralism to multilateralism.

2. In the context of the global power struggle, new options and potentially new or redefined blocs have arisen.

3. The OBOR project is both an economic structural measure and an expression of the implicit claim to power of China and the emerging countries.

The Eurasian Economic Union (EAEU) is an association of five countries in the North East of Eurasia that have formed an internal market with a customs union. The economic union emerged from the Eurasian Economic Community, which came into effect on January 1, 2015.

The founding agreement was signed on May 29, 2014 by Kazakhstan, Russia and Belarus. An accession agreement was signed with Armenia on October 10, 2014. Kyrgyzstan joined the Union on August 12, 2015. The aim of the Eurasian Economic Union is to facilitate the exchange of goods, capital, services and labor. In addition, five additional countries wish to coordinate parts of their economic policies on the model of the European Union: Tajikistan is now a Candidate country, and Uzbekistan, Mongolia, Azerbaijan, and Syria are now potential candidates.

Aims of the EAEU

The EAEU follows the model of the European Union. It's aims include: abolition of customs duties and customs controls (customs union); single economic space (2007); free movement of persons, goods and services, and capital flows (January 1, 2015); common market for pharmaceutical goods and medical devices (January 1, 2016); the beginning of a common energy market and a common electricity market (2019); a common oil market (2024); a common gas market (2025); creating the conditions for a single financial market, a common currency (by 2025).

Economic and Structural Data

RUSSIA

GDP growth for 2018: About 2%.

Consumer prices currently: 2.4% year on year.

Foreign trade: Surplus of about $10 billion per month.

Real wage increase: Currently ca. 7% year on year.

Public budget: Deficit of 0% of the GDP for 2018, according to IMF forecast.

Public debt: 18.7% of the GDP, according to IMF forecast.

BELARUS

Economic development: Turnaround carried out.

Investment: Moderate rise expected.

Consumption: Private consumption could rise by 3% in 2018.

Foreign trade: Strong growth of German exports in 2017.

Economic growth in 2017 mainly supported industry, which was able to increase its output in real terms by 6.3% in the first eleven months. Belarus profited from the economic recovery in Russia as its most important export market, and from the rise in raw material prices. After the declines of previous years, exports rose sharply in 2017. After settling the dispute with Russia over oil and gas supplies in April, deliveries of oil and gas and thus production in the highly important petrochemical industry of Belarus picked up again. Further impulses came from the service sector and agriculture. In contrast, the construction industry remained negative.

KAZAKHSTAN

Investment: Strong growth in the coming years is expected.

Investment will continue to be strong. From 2018 to 2022, the government expects gross investment to grow an average of 7.2% per year; the 2017 growth is expected to come in at 4.7%. Government spending on industrial and infrastructure projects, as well as increased investments from the People's Republic of China, account for most of the investment.

ARMENIA

Economic development: Good chances for strong growth in 2018.

Investment: Long-expected turnaround in sight.

Consumption: Consumer spending is again on the rise.

Foreign trade: Good perspectives for further significant growth.

The national debt is increasing. Government-owned foreign debt is expected to reach 60% of GDP by the end of 2018, compared with 55.1% in 2017 (estimate) and 44.2% in 2015. The country's poverty rate is nearly 30%. Forced and sustainable economic development, and above all, the efficient integration of Armenia into international cooperation, is considerably hampered by the closed borders with its neighbors, Azerbaijan and Turkey, as a result of the unresolved geopolitical conflict over the Nagorno-Karabakh region.

KIRGYZSTAN

Economic development: The pace slowed down due to a decline in gold mining.

Investment: International donors and Chinese investors are decisive.

Consumption: Income development looks good.

Foreign trade: Imports growing strongly.

The GDP of Kirgyzstan rose by 1.3% between January and April 2018, much slower than one year earlier. The main reason is the decline in gold mining in the Kumtor Mine, the country's economic heavyweight. Otherwise, the economic engine was not running smoothly everywhere. Excluding Kumtor, GDP growth remained modest at 2.5% during the reporting period.

However, the prospects are good. After a plus of 4.6% in the previous year, the GDP could even increase by 4.2% in 2018 according to the World Bank.

From January to April 2018, construction, services and agriculture contributed positively to GDP growth. In addition, the Kyrgyz economy will benefit not only from the fast-paced development in China, but also from the economic recovery in two other important partner countries, Russia and Kazakhstan.

DUŠKO DIMITRIJEVIĆ

New Silk Road: Achievements & Prospects Of Serbia-China Economic Cooperation

Duško Dimitrijević, PhD, is a Professorial Fellow, Institute of International Politics and Economics, Serbia. He spoke on Panel IV of the Schiller Institute conference on July 1, 2018. This is an edited transcript of his presentation.

Ladies and Gentlemen, *guten Tag, bonjour, dobry dan* [Russian], *ni hao* [Chinese]. [laughter]

You Excellencies, ladies and gentlemen, distinguished organizers, it's my special honor and pleasure to greet you and to thank you for your kind invitation to participate in this conference for a world order of peace

Duško Dimitrijević

based on the development of nations, prepared by the distinguished Schiller Institute. I wish to express special gratitude to Mr. Lyndon LaRouche and Mrs. Helga Zepp-LaRouche, founder and president of this famous temple of wisdom; as well as to my colleagues Mrs. Elke Fimmen and Mr. Klaus Fimmen. Today's lecture, which I prepared for this occasion, deals with a very interesting topic on the achievements and prospects of the economic cooperation between China and Serbia, in the context of One Belt, One Road. As the old Romans said, *scripta manent* [spoken words fly away, written words remain]. I prepared something and I will read it for you.

China's Development Strategy

China's development strategy of the New Silk Road, with the two framework initiatives known as One Belt, One Road, *Yi Dai Yi Lu*, which was announced by the Chinese President Xi Jinping in 2013, provides for long-term improvement of relations especially with the countries of Asia, Europe, and Africa. This strategy represents an ideological concept of the Chinese foreign policy that aims to uphold world peace and to promote common and harmonious development of the whole world. In contrast to the geopolitical strategies of the great powers that is mainly based on the divisive approaches, the Chinese New Silk Road focusses on common interests and cooperation in order to achieve mutual benefits.

With an open-door policy applied for more than three decades, China is trying to strengthen its position in international politics, and to contribute to an active participation in the globalization process, in order to achieve these goals which are formulated through the motto, "Chinese dream." China is constantly changing on the social plane, repeatedly carrying out economic reforms and building a new vision of international relations based on the promotion of political, economic, and cultural cooperation and social progress between different nations and different states, building a so-called "community of common interests, destiny and responsibility" or, in other words, "a community of shared future for mankind."

Hence, despite significant geopolitical changes after the Cold War, a strong political influence in the international process, and expressed opportunism in international relations, China has continued to act as an abiding factor in solving major international problems, using as a model the Five Principles of Peaceful Coexistence, the Panchsheel Principles, which is in line with the purposes and principles of the United Nations Charter.

As the world's second largest economy with nearly one-fifth of the world's population, China has committed herself to expanding good relations with other countries, especially with the developing countries, such as Serbia.

Serbia-China Relations

In geopolitical terms, Serbia is located in Southeast Europe at the crossroads linking the Black Sea and the North Sea, and Southeastern Europe to Central and

Western Europe. Its territory is small and landlocked, with limited political, economic, social and demographic capacity. Serbia is a militarily neutral and defense-oriented state. As one of the successor states to the former Yugoslavia, Serbia has a mixed national identity, and a mixed cultural and historical heritage, which in international relations makes it a much more open and accountable partner.

Traditionally, Serbia has had good relations with the main actors in international politics. As a member of the United Nations and other major international organizations, Serbia is trying to build good relations with other countries and to promote peace, stability, equality and mutual trust. In Serbia's actual foreign policy strategy, the People's Republic of China occupies an important place. Serbia's strategy is expressed by its four pillars of foreign policy.

The first pillar is the European Union, whose member Serbia would like to become; second pillar is Russia, as a world political rising power, and historical partner of Serbia; the third pillar is the United States, as a great power, with whom Serbia has had fluctuating relations in the past, but whose importance and influence in international relations Serbia has accepted as a reality; and the fourth important pillar of Serbian foreign policy strategy is China, as a global economic power and traditionally a good friend of Serbia in international relations.

Relations between Serbia and China have followed the continuity of relations between Yugoslavia and the People's Republic of China that commenced with its recognition of China on October 1, 1949. China's foreign policy and security concept is based on principles of sovereignty and territorial integrity of states, advocating cooperation of equality and mutual benefit, and non-interference in the national affairs of other countries. Since the two countries encourage friendly relations with each other and actively participate in development through various forms of bilateral and multilateral cooperation, at the regional, sub-regional, and global level, it can be said that these relations have become of prime and strategic importance.

Xinhua/Li Tao

Chinese President Xi Jinping (L) and Serbian President Tomislav Nikolić attend a signing ceremony of a joint statement to lift bilateral relationship of China and Serbia to comprehensive strategic partnership, Serbia, June 18, 2016.

How China Views South and East Europe

Today, it is much clearer than yesterday, that China is a very important Asian economic partner of Serbia, and one of the major pillars of Serbia's foreign policy. On the other hand, Serbia is one of the key Chinese partners in the region of South and East Europe. China primarily sees South and East Europe in terms of economic integration with the European Union, as a common market of high purchasing power, and therefore an ideal space for the placement of its own products. In this regard, it is important to note that China supports Serbia's aspiration for full accession to the EU without prejudice to its vital national interests.

At this point, it is worth mentioning that Serbia was granted candidate status for membership in the EU on March 1, 2012. With this new status, Serbia has taken a significant step towards the European common market, with the prospect for achieving real economic growth and social development.

For economic and social transformation of Serbia, China could also play a decisive role, because it does not pursue geostrategic redesigning of the European area, but seeks to maintain the stability of the existing order. This is the best thing through China's seat on the

UN Security Council, where it's committed to preservation of the territorial integrity of Serbia. On the other hand, Serbia supports the territorial integrity of China, its sovereignty and its right to regulate its relations with the former separate parts of its territory through the Chinese foreign policy, its One China policy.

Cooperation between the two countries is now at the highest level since the establishment of diplomatic relations in 1955, and each day is expanding with new positive content. In view of this affirmation, Serbia's position toward China and its role in Chinese development strategy, the New Silk Road, are determined by many factors.

As is well known, Sino-Serbian relations are characterized by the strategic partnership established in August 2009, with the joint statement of then President Boris Tadić and Hu Jintao. This strategic partnership was expanded to a comprehensive strategic partnership through the joint statement of Serbian and Chinese Presidents Tomislav Nikolić and Xi Jinping, signed in August 2013, and in June 2016. In view of these facts, a series of framework agreements on political and economic cooperation has been concluded. For example, the agreement on economic and technical cooperation in the field of infrastructure, signed in August 2009, paved the way for the many other joint projects in the fields of energy sectors, transport, agriculture, telecommunication, finance and cultural exchange.

The 16+1 Mechanism

The importance of these projects and their profitability can only be understood in the context of implementation of the Chinese development strategy, which includes the objective of previously formulated global strategy which China has encouraged its companies to exploit in the world markets. Hence, the Serbian position towards China's development strategy depends on the understanding of global processes in the world, and geo-economic interests of China that are channeled through the mechanism 16+1, which represents a political platform for cooperation between China and the countries of Central and Eastern Europe. Because the cooperation mechanism 16+1 is in line with the Chinese objective of being a partner for growth with the EU, its relationship with the Central and Eastern European countries may be a growth driver within the framework of China-EU relations.

China believes that by enhancing the overall level of its relations with the Central and Eastern European countries it will be in a position to promote a more stable and healthy China-Europe relationship as well. Such an approach presupposes harmonization of both the Central and Eastern European countries and their national development strategies, respecting their legal frameworks; and then, also respecting the authority, rules and standards of the EU, as well as complying with the obligations agreed to in the strategic documents such as Agenda 2020, whose implementation could be of crucial importance for the sustainable success of cooperation with the framework of the 16+1 mechanisms.

As Serbia is an active participant in the cooperation mechanism 16+1, it could also be a good partner in the realization of the Chinese development strategy and it's One Belt, One Road initiative, which promotes cooperation between different countries and peoples of different regions and from different continents. This can best be demonstrated through the analysis of Sino-Serbian economic achievement.

Although Serbia views China as its most important strategic partner in Asia, its economic relations with China are characterized by mutual asymmetry in all economic parameters. But regarding these parameters, it does not mean that there are no real possibilities for their further growth and development. China sees Serbia as a key partner in the region of Southeast Europe, as well as an active actor in the way of connecting with the European Union, whose common market, with high purchasing power, can be an ideal place for investment and the placement of products. In this sense, China supports Serbia's aspiration, as I said, for full membership in this organization.

Good political relations with China provide Serbia with the opportunity to develop good economic relations with her in different ways and in different fields. Currently, economic cooperation on its [inaudible] value and structure, unfortunately makes up only a small part of the economic exchange with the world in both countries. This state of affairs is primarily conditioned by the Chinese economic strategy, whose constants are global geo-economic positioning; growing expansion of exports; acquisition of energy and mining resources for the purpose of maintaining economic growth; and significant logistical and financial support of state structures and state banks for companies operating abroad.

In those pursuits, China is emerging as a major investor worldwide; it is therefore clear that economic cooperation with China is a major economic challenge and incentive for Serbia. However, the two countries have a clear will to improve their economic relations, which is best reflected through the Chinese foreign direct investments (FDI) in Serbian transport, infrastructure, energy, and ICT [information and communication technology] sectors. According to official data, the main Chinese project investments in Serbia's economy have reached a level of around $6 billion.

Serbia Seeks a Role in Global Value Chains

Hence, economic cooperation with China represents a huge opportunity for development, and also provides good evidence of successful conduct of foreign policy, which promotes cooperation on the global level and contributes to the constructive meeting of East and West. However, if Serbia wants to increase its influence and importance in international relations based on economic cooperation with China, its business with China must be based not only on past success and achievements, but also on improving its real economic capacity, through the various types of investments. In industry infrastructure, in this sense, Serbia will have to successfully involve itself in international production through the global value chains which derive not only from proprietary invest-

Zhang Dejiang, chairman of the Standing Committee of China's National People's Congress (NPC), visits a steel mill during his official visit to Serbia, July 17, 2017.

ments, but also from portfolio investments.

Serbia can be included in this chain in two ways: First, through foreign direct investments, by which the Chinese party acquires ownership rights but also control over Serbian companies. For example, through the establishment of a brand new company through greenfield investments; or through investments in the realization of capacity of existing ones through brownfield investments; or through joint ventures and international mergers and acquisitions, where companies from China and Serbia establish new companies; or by Chinese purchase of Serbian companies in order to acquire property and business connections. Second, through indirect investments that represent the purchase of securities by the Chinese party for the purpose of investing capital in Serbian companies, without the intention of directly influencing their business policy.

In these ways, the Serbian economy could be included in the global value chains through Chinese investment capital, and Serbian companies could realize long-term benefits from the export of products and services that would be owned by Chinese and Chinese-Serbian companies.

It is quite certain that were the Serbian economy to be included in the global value

Zhang Dejiang, chairman of the Standing Committee of China's National People's Congress (NPC), visits a power station during his visit to Serbia, July 17, 2017.

chain through Chinese investment capital, Serbian companies could realize a prosperous export benefit whose carriers were Chinese or mixed Chinese-Serbian firms. This could lead to the further expansion of mutual economic cooperation, but also to the linking of a number of countries from the Central and Eastern European region to the Chinese-Serbian investment project.

That these possibilities are realistic is also due to the fact that Serbia has adopted appropriate economic policy measures and has provided a solid legal framework as guarantee for the Chinese foreign investments. In this regard, it is important that Serbia has continuously renewed and developed its bilateral investment arrangements with China. Such a good example is the case which happened during the visit of Chinese President Xi Jinping to Serbia in June 2016. The two sides signed a new agreement of economic and technical cooperation with 20 other agreements and legal instruments of cooperation in different fields.

A Stable, Legally Transparent Business Arena

The need for permanent legal security of foreign investors in Serbia has led Serbia to adopt model investment goals, which guarantee equal legal status for domestic and foreign investors. Regardless of the form of foreign investments, or acquisition of shares in existing enterprises, the establishment of new companies, franchises, BOT [build, operate, transfer] arrangements, concessions and other business transactions, Serbian law as from 2015 guarantees freedom of investments, national treatment, legal certainty, and the ability to transfer profits abroad.

The further development of economic cooperation between Serbia and China, entailed the examination of comparative advantages that Serbia has and can contribute, to increase the structure and scope of Chinese investments. These benefits include some of the following factors: a clear foreign policy goal, relative macroeconomic stability; a highly-qualified and relatively cheap labor force; regionally competitive financial risk; a privatized banking sector; rapid development of capital markets; development of telecommunications infrastructure; a liberalized system of tariffs and tax legislation; the rapid development of the private sector; a significant level of income; fiscal regulatory and financial measures; the existence of free trade agreements with the European Union, CEFTA, AFTA, Russia, Belarus, Turkey, Kazakhstan and other countries; the adoption of a national strategy for promotion and development of foreign investments; and full visa liberalization between China and Serbia.

Conclusion

So, let me conclude: As history shows, each country must follow world trends in order to achieve its prosperity; otherwise it will be out of the world. The question is then, "What are the current trends?" For China, this is definitely peace, development, cooperation, and mutual progress. China does not accept the models of international relations based on imperialism, neocolonialism, and hegemony.

As I mentioned earlier, one of our presenters said China stands for multilateralism in international relations and for a multipolar world order in which peaceful development has no alternative. Therefore, it's understandable why China's new development strategy of the New Silk Road emphasizes the full historical momentum for the progressive development of the whole of humanity, and why China promotes the open-minded ideas of the new normal, which deepens the earlier ideological concept of global economic development and reform of international society into the community of common interests, destiny and peaceful stability.

Hence, in my opinion, it's indeed a prophetic statement from the esteemed Mrs. Helga Zepp-LaRouche, that the New Silk Road—which becomes the World Land-Bridge and is the basis for the peace order for the 21st Century—requires a New Paradigm of thinking. This New Paradigm can only be one that proceeds from the common aims of mankind. These aims of mankind can be achieved exclusively through the dialogue between different civilizations. In this regard, I repeat the words of the Chinese President, Xi Jinping:

> Countries may have differences and even encounter problems with each other, which is to be expected. But we should not forget that we all live under the same sky, share one and the same home planet, and belong to one and the same family. People across the world should be guided by the vision that all the people under Heaven are of one family, embrace each other with open arms, enhance mutual understanding, and seek common ground while setting aside differences. Together we should endeavor to build a community with a shared future of mankind.

Thank you very much.

HANS VON HELLDORFF

Necessary Regulatory Framework for Investments of German/European SME Economy Along the New Silk Road

Hans von Helldorff is the Spokesman for the Federal Association of the German Silk Road Initiative (BVDSI). This is an edited version of his prepared text. He spoke on Panel IV of the Schiller Institute conference, on July 1, 2018.

China's One Belt, One Road (OBOR) initiative can unquestionably be described as the greatest global investment program ever, so far. Projects worth $900 billion which are now under construction, as well as other planned projects with a volume of close to $4 trillion, leave no doubt as to how serious China's intention is, to become the leading economic power on Earth.

Hans von Helldorff

Of course, one can discuss whether China intends to pursue hegemonic goals, or whether it is only seeking to give an unprecedented dynamic to global development for the benefit of many. What is sure, is that China is not just giving anything away, and, yes, China, too, is acting primarily in its own interest.

The longstanding stable growth of the Chinese economy has led to a change in the role and the self-conception of China's economic and foreign policy. A closer look shows that the shift from the role of a workbench to a leading technological power is not surprising.

Although initial successes in terms of know-how transfer to high technology qualifications were still based in the early days on joint ventures or partly also on the unauthorized adaptation of intellectual property of western companies, since the middle of the 1980s, China has consistently and outstandingly invested in training, research and technology. Tens of thousands of students have been sent to prestigious universities around the world and, after successful studies, have been given good positions in their own economy.

Together with massive support for industry and a successful monetary and financial policy, this strategy has paid off. China's massive foreign exchange reserves have not only allowed it to become the largest creditor of the United States, but also to become the foundation of an unstoppable, highly expansive international economic policy. The greatest manifestation of that currently is the OBOR initiative.

From the perspective of our association, One Belt One Road is the strategic gateway to a new, more just world economic order. But it is also an opportunity and an offer for the German economy to bring to bear its enormous capabilities and its excellent reputation. Unfortunately, this point of view is scarcely to be found in German and EU politics. Instead, the skeptics dominate. With a strange mixture of arguments, they claim the authority to interpret and assess Chinese intentions and omissions. This attitude has led to much irritation in Asian countries, in Russia and certain EU member countries, such as Hungary, Greece and the Czech Republic, just to name a few.

Germany a Tolerated Onlooker?

The premises of German foreign and economic policy are based more on ideal and moral values, such as human rights and more democracy. In other words, Germany's interests, as the strongest exporting nation in the world, come last. That leads to a decoupling of political speed from economic speed. Germany thus runs the risk within a short time of jeopardizing its position as a leading economic nation and being reduced to playing the role of a tolerated onlooker. This unilateral orientation to values and to the West has not produced any sensible results in the recent past.

To take just one example, Germany and the EU approved the extension of sanctions against Russia. Russia has enough options on its own or in partnerships to handle these sanctions. But the alternatives of the German economy, on the contrary, are clear. Trade of goods and services with Russia has noticeably decreased. Even if we ignore that, the problem remains of the difficult rebuilding of trust between the EU and Russia.

The point I want to make is the following: The game of economic policy forces is now very dynamic and requires a constant adjustment of one's own doctrine and foreign trade objectives, for example. These demands, however, require a government that has a clear view of necessities. In addition, these demands require a government that is able to formulate policies clearly and precisely, and if necessary, with a vision. Unfortunately, these skills have been steadily declining in Germany since 1983.

Dealing with problems so detailed that they do not belong in the Bundestag, has led to a loss in credibility of Germany's major parties. If we translate this situation and its results onto the challenges that face us in Europe, doubts will quickly arise as to whether and how German policy will manage to address the OBOR project on an equal footing. What's more, how should German small and medium-sized business (SMEs) have confidence that the necessary regulatory framework will be found, or perhaps created, with the help and active support of the countries along the Silk Road. In the economies along the traditional Silk Road alone, there is an enormous demand, for example, for infrastructure projects, energy projects, the development of medium-sized industrial clusters, training projects, health projects, etc.

The opportunities for the German economy are enormous. We in the BVDSI, in the many conversations we have with the ambassadors of these countries, have all found that the desire for German participation in the framework of China's OBOR investments is constantly growing. It is driven by confidence in German technology, in German management methods, in our cooperative business culture and innovative ability.

SMEs' Need to Navigate Safe Waters on OBOR

But to come back to the core challenges for the German Mittelstand economy. As you probably know, Germany has a very strong medium-sized economy, which is also largely made up of family businesses.

This strong nucleus of the German economy has produced an enormous amount of "hidden champions" in almost all branches of the world market. This middle-sized economy is the secret of our country's export success and its innovation and investment capabilities. The major DAX [Frankfurt Stock Exchange Index] companies are not the ones that absolutely need political support. They are well represented everywhere and can assert their interests all by themselves.

No, it is the medium-sized family businesses that need political support. These family-owned companies need to navigate, from a regulatory standpoint, in relatively safe waters. That includes bi- or multinational agreements on the protection of investments and the protection of intellectual property. This includes clear, understandable measures against corruption and state arbitrariness. It also includes guarantees for the free movement of goods and capital. Last but not least, regulations must be established to guarantee safety in terms of claims settlement and compensation. Special export and project financing is another area of support services that must be put in place for OBOR.

Fortunately, there are already examples of the creation of an important regulatory framework. Kazakhstan has created an impressive legal landscape, which corresponds in many areas to German legislation. Russia has created extensive guarantee packages and arbitration boards with which the German businessmen active in Russia feel to a great extent comfortable.

However, there remains a lot to do, especially in the areas of corruption and arbitrariness of public authorities. The EU and Germany have vast experience in developing, contracting and codifying such regulations and procedures. They come from the accession agreements to the EU as well as from bilateral agreements. So it's not because of a lack of know-how that the necessary political dynamic is not yet recognizable. Here, a new spirit is urgently needed.

In all agreements to be made with the countries of the Silk Road, in all dignified interests of the parties, one thing must be clear for Germany and for the EU: it is not about demarcation or confrontation with the OBOR initiative. Only a cooperative approach ensures perspectives. It's about participation, prosperity and partnership.

Germany has the duty, both internally and externally, to take up new global initiatives. Otherwise, we will lose our opportunity in Europe to participate in shaping a new world economic order.

The Eurasian Canal and the New Silk Road

Professor Nuraly Bekturganov is the Vice President of the National Academy of Natural Sciences of the Republic of Kazakhstan. This is an edited transcript of the English translation of his presentation, by video, on Panel IV of the Schiller Institute conference, on July 1, 2018.

I am Nuraly Sultanovich Bekturganov, representing the National Academy of Natural Sciences of the Republic of Kazakhstan. We are a community of scientists in Kazakhstan.

Together with scientists from Russia and China, we have conducted a series of investigations to assist in pushing forward the construction of a canal and hydroelectric station. The completion of the canal was halted in 1941, due to the start of World War II. In total, approximately 396 km of earth was dug, out of the 750 km needed for the entire canal.

The idea of constructing such a canal connecting the Caspian and Black seas has a very long history, which had been largely associated with political and military applications. Originating in the last century, it was called the Manych Waterway and was designed in the second half of the 1930s. The Ust-Manych hydroelectric complex was built in 1936. In 1941, the Veselovsky and Proletarskiy hydro-schemes were developed, which were aligned with the same reservoirs. However, further design and construction work on the canal was abruptly interrupted by the Second World War.

About 15,000 years ago, during the last Ice Age, that is, when the ice caps started to melt, the water level of the Caspian Sea was about 100 meters higher than it is now. By way of this Manych Waterway, water has traditionally flowed from the Caspian into the Black Sea. But after all these years, the situation has changed somewhat dramatically. Now, the water level of the Caspian is much lower than that of the Black Sea, about 27 meters lower. That is, over a distance of about 750 km between the Caspian and the Black Sea, the water level drops

Professor Nuraly Bekturganov

about 27 meters. Only about six locks would be necessary in order for cargo ships to speed through a canal between the two seas.

Nazarbayev and Putin Support the Canal

Such a canal itself would traverse the Kalmykia region of Russia, to the Rostov region of Russia. Construction of such a canal has been discussed numerous times, by both the Presidents of Kazakhstan and Russia. Here's what President Nazarbayev, one of the initiators of the Eurasian canal commission, had to say about it:

We are in need of different routes: Naturally these goods (oil and gas) would go along those routes which prove to be more economically viable for us. A major project along these lines could be the construction of the new—Eurasian—shipping canal which stretches from the Caspian to the Black Sea.

And here's President of the Russian Federation Vladimir Vladimirovich Putin:

The emergence of a new canal will not only give the states in the Caspian region access to the Black and Mediterranean Seas, that is, to the world's oceans, but will also change for the better their geopolitical positions, allowing them to become maritime powers.

Of course, we have seen an initiative coming from the leader of the People's Republic of China, Xi Jinping. Since 2013 he's been actively pushing what the Chinese are calling the One Belt, One Road. The Eurasian Silk Road Canal is also an initiative. The Eurasian Canal is shorthand for the Nurly Zhol project, a Russian strategic transportation project. When combined, these projects will create a multimodal transit corridor run-

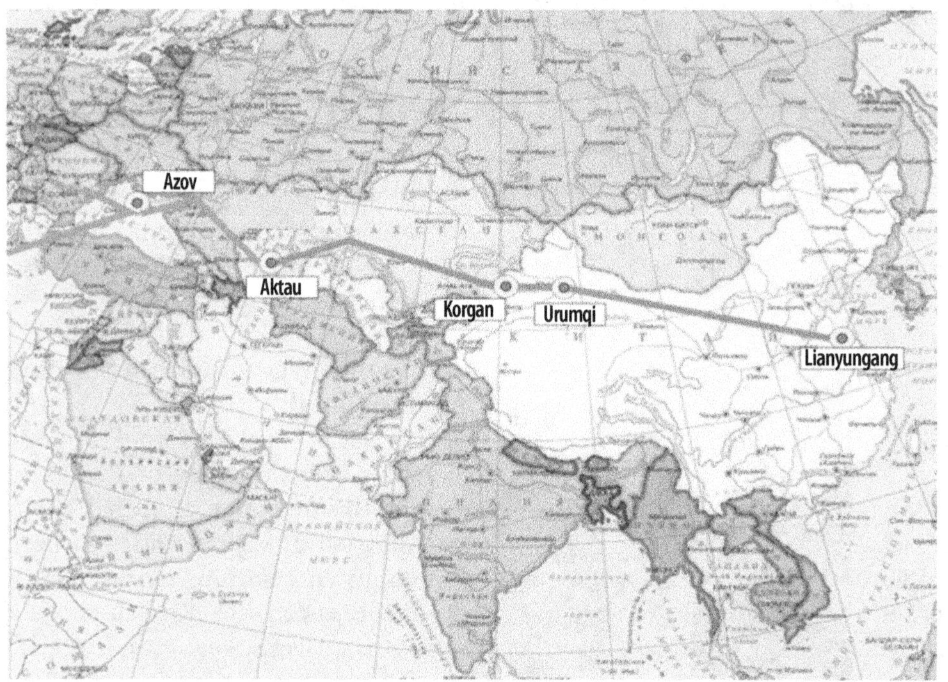

ning through the territory of China, Kazakhstan, and Russia, along the routes following the Lianyungang Port (China), Korgan and Dostyk, Aktau Port (Kazakhstan), through the Eurasian Canal and into the Azov-Black Sea Basin (Russia).

The distance along the Chinese portion comes to about 3,300 km; in Kazakhstan, it's about 2,200 km; and in Russia, it's about 1,800 km. These distances compare with other routes along the Eurasian Silk Road Canal from China, Kazakhstan, and Russia. More than one million people live in the local communities in and around the canal corridors in Central Asia and the Far East. All these people, and their families, will benefit through employment and other services brought to the region by way of this project.

Survey Data Supports Construction

The realization of the Eurasian Silk Road Canal project is also oriented to the current delivery of goods for Kazakhstan by way of this transport canal. We reviewed the amount of goods being transported from China to Europe and found that its implementation will entail redirecting a significant part of the ocean trade turnover between Europe and China, which today passes through the Suez Canal. According to calculations provided by the Sinohydro Corporation, a Chinese company, upon implementing the Silk Road via the Eurasian Canal project, by 2030, some 20-25 mil-

lion tons of Chinese exports now delivered via the Suez Canal route could be delivered along the Eurasian Canal route; and by 2050, close to about 34-44 million tons of Chinese goods could be delivered this way.

The transportation infrastructure of the People's Republic of China is already ready to transport this quantity of cargo via "the Silk Road via the Eurasian Canal," in line with affordable tariffs for EU member states.

After considering these data, as well as data collected by specialists in and around the Caspian regions, we also calculated that upon completion of the Eurasian Canal, by the year 2050, cargo of about 120 million tons per year could be delivered along this route. This number is already comparable to the amount of goods being delivered via the Panama Canal.

Arguments Against Construction Refuted

In 2008-2010, we conducted a comparative assessment of the technical and economic characteristics of construction projects of a new navigable canal linking the Caspian and Black seas. In the process, we reviewed a few arguments against its building. The main argument we encountered was based on an absence of an economically viable cargo flow, basing their assumptions on a comparison with the Volga-Don2 canal, in which the cargo load was calculated at only 3.5 million tons—10 times less than our calculations! We concluded that this argument could really no longer be used.

We also looked at the number of freight trains travelling between China and Europe and the volume of cargo carried in each direction. To this day, interestingly, no one but us has really ever considered discussing this as applied to the Eurasian Canal!

Up until 2014, that is, prior to the launch of the One Belt, One Road initiative, container cargo from Europe to China was practically nonexistent, but by 2014, 28 trains returned to China, loaded with goods, and in

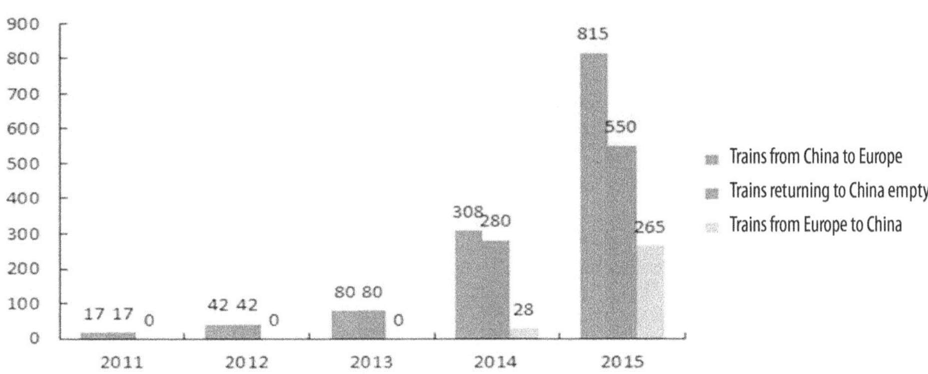

2015, out of 815 trains sent west from China, 265 returned loaded with cargo, an increase of 10 fold. And if we consider 2016, the amount of cargo coming into China doubled, coming to about 52,000 containers a year. The problem of under-loaded containers coming from Europe to China by land becomes less severe than by sea. According to the latest data, every second container is filled from Europe to China, travelling by land, and every third container is filled, travelling by sea. This is, of course, already a very good reason for building the Eurasian Canal.

We encountered a second argument against building the Eurasian Canal: In April 2015, the leader of the People's Republic of China, President Xi Jinping, signed an investment agreement in Pakistan, to invest $46 billion towards the construction of the "Kashgar-Gwadar" transportation corridor. Completion of this project will provide the western and central regions of the People's Republic of China with a cheap multimodal outlet to the world's oceans.

Eurasian transit through the territory of Kazakhstan and Russia must be competitive with this K-G corridor, possible only with the construction of the Eurasian Canal. Otherwise, after completion of the Kashgar-Gwadar project, Russia and Kazakhstan lose, even in terms of today's cargo volume. This is one more reason why it's necessary to speed up the process of building the Eurasian Canal.

The Canal Benefits All Countries En Route

Question: "How would constructing the Eurasian Canal benefit Kazakhstan?" According to recent figures, Kazakhstan would gain significant revenues from the transit of goods through its territory. Today, with the transportation of 18 million tons of cargo, Kazakhstan earns more than $1 billion. Completion of the Eurasian Silk Road Canal, as I already mentioned, will attract another 20-25 million tons of Chinese export cargo by 2030, and another 34-44 million tons by 2050, which would provide an additional annual income of $1.9 billion by 2030, and $2.4 billion by 2050.

The best argument for the construction, or the completion, of the Eurasian Canal, I believe, is this: transport of offshore oil from the Caspian Sea. Over the last four years, the largest oil deposits in the world have been discovered in what's called the offshore Kashagan oil deposit, located in the north end of the Caspian Sea, an area which belongs to Kazakhstan. Over the last 13 years, some of the world's biggest oil corporations have been actively investing—companies such as Total, ENI, ExxonMobil, Chinese national oil companies, Kazakh national oil companies. After a colossal amount of money spent on the opening of this offshore site, it is now ready to start production.

But there's the question of how to deliver the crude to consumers. Of course, the idea of using pipelines is very attractive. However, if the Eurasian Canal is com-

Kashagan off-shore oil field.

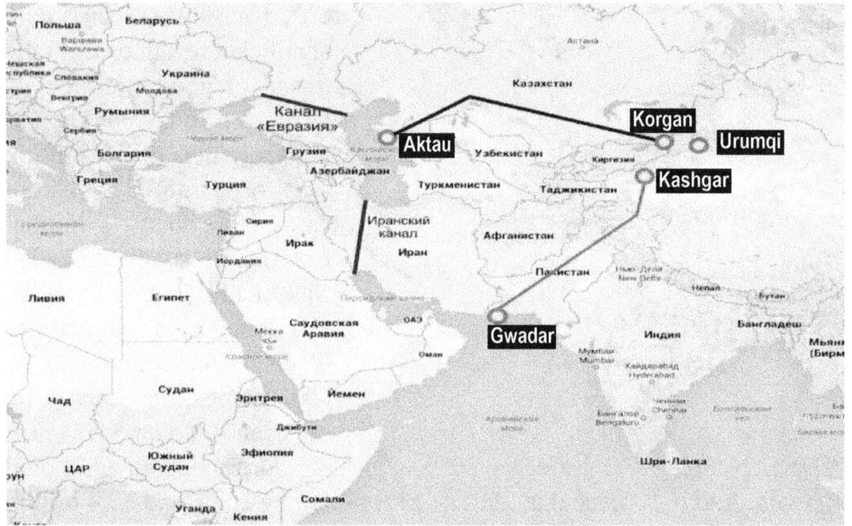

pleted, ships could deliver the crude to consumers by way of the ocean. The production of crude oil from Kashagan would bring a huge benefit, especially when you consider that the greatest peak of oil extraction from this offshore site could amount to about 75 million tons of oil in the near future. That is, in addition to the 25 million tons of goods flowing through the Eurasian Canal, we would also have cargo of an initial 75 million tons of oil extracted through the Kashagan offshore facility. So this is a very serious argument in favor of the construction of the Eurasian Canal.

In order to start up the canal project again, we conducted a few investigations on the integrated technical and economic indicators surrounding its construction and operation. In accordance with Russian standards, we studied the geographical conditions, the terrain surrounding the canal that would go through Russian territory. We also studied the route it would take in Kazakhstan, gathering reliable data on the physiographical, engineering-geological, and seismic-tectonic conditions. We produced a collection of maps, covering the main aspects of the natural environment (terrain, geotechnical conditions, climate, water resources, soils, vegetation) in ArcGIS 10. We compiled maps over the buffer zone, defined by increments of 25 km. Numerical models of the terrain along the routes have also been constructed. All these various factors we published in our book, which I'll be glad to present you at the end of my presentation.

Traffic and Cargo Analysis

Chinese specialists from the Sinohydro company also conducted a number of experiments on a complex number of physical factors surrounding the canal, along the Chinese route from Lianyungang to Khorgos.

All of this has been prepared in order to assist in speeding up the restarting of construction. Over the last three years, many scientists in Kazakhstan, Russia and China have conducted a lot of additional scientific investigations into the construction of the Eurasian Canal. In addition, numerous analyses were conducted on the cargo that would be transported through it, for example oil, as well as all the Chinese goods. By 2050, calculations show, the cargo load could amount to 120 million tons, and with the Kashagan oil, that could bring the load up to 200 million tons a year. This means that the cargo that would flow through the canal would be massive.

It was suggested to us to dig a parallel canal alongside the 1941 hydro-station canal, which is only about 5-6 meters deep, and basically considered to be able to handle no more than 10,000 tons of cargo. We suggested deepening the canal to about 11.5 meters. If built to a depth of about 8 meters, the amount of cargo that would be able to flow through would be more 50,000 tons. But if we deepen to about 10-11 meters, then the ships would be able to carry more than 100,000 tons.

Our most important suggestion, however, was to line the canal with concrete. This would make it easier to control the water through the canal, as well as resolve any issues surrounding the local eco-system, as the 1941 canal has caused. The new technology we have today could be used to monitor and minimize water usage, therefore answering another criticism of the canal by some ecologists who say that the canal would degrade and disrupt the local eco-system.

Construction of the Eurasian Canal would elevate the standing of the regions of the Caspian where approximately 1 million people live, and would allow them to take part in the world's waterway transportation systems.

Conclusion

To conclude, "the Silk Road via the Eurasian Canal" is well-timed, of immediate interest to the global community, and has tremendous prospect of practical implementation in the near future.

All of our recent findings are published in a book

written about the Eurasian Silk Road Canal project, under the general editorship of the President of the National Academy of Sciences, Nurtai Abykayevich Abykayev. All of our findings are printed in that publication.

Allow me to thank, of course, Dean Andromidas, who, in his article on the Eurasian Canal, was the only one who finally made note of our article titled, "The Eurasian Canal As a Factor of Economic Prosperity for the Caspian Region." This is one of ten different publications that we have on the Eurasian Canal. Thanks to Dean, we also met Michael and Meghan, and Jason and Alicia, all of whom enabled us to voice the findings we gathered with the assistance of the scientific communities in Kazakhstan, Russia and China.

Thank you very much for your attention.

AMBASSADOR LEONIDAS CHRYSANTHOPOULOS

The Integration of the Eurasian Continent

Leonidas Chrysanthopoulos is a former Greek Ambassador and was the Secretary General of the Black Sea Economic Cooperation Organization. This is an edited version of his prepared text. He spoke on Panel IV of the Schiller Institute Conference, on July 1, 2018.

I would like to start by quoting my conclusion from the paper I submitted to last year's International Scientific Conference that was held in Belgrade on the initiatives of the New Silk Road.

Leonidas Chrysanthopoulos

East, while the perspectives that open for humanity—scientific, cultural, philosophical, and spiritual—with global peace prevailing, are immense. This is why the Belt and Road Initiative must succeed.

The successful implementation of the Belt and Road Initiative could, in the long run, unite the overlapping regional organizations and initiatives in Asia, in one major organization that would have as its epicenter, the Belt and Road.

In conclusion, if this project that is of paramount importance to humanity is to succeed, peace and stability must prevail. However, the existence and promotion of this project can also facilitate successful peace initiatives if the parties in conflict are able to understand that their benefits from their participation in the Belt and Road Initiative greatly surpass ambiguous benefits from prevailing in a conflict. Such was the experience with the Black Sea Ring Highway, where differences between some BSEC [Black Sea Economic Cooperation] member states were able to be softened to the extent that the highway was allowed to pass through zones of frozen conflicts.

Consequently, a successful Belt and Road Initiative is by itself an incentive for pacification. One can only imagine how Asia would be with peace in Afghanistan and in the Middle

Problems the BRI Has To Overcome

I will expand a little on the problems that the BRI has to face in order to succeed. I will start first with the EU, an organization that no longer has any contact with the people of Europe, an organization that has done away with democratic procedures, an organization that is destroying its members. The EU does not like this initiative at all, which ends within its territory, and is to its benefit.

In April the EU ambassadors in Beijing issued a report that criticized the BRI, since it runs counter to the EU agenda for liberalizing trade and pushes the balance of power in favor of Chinese-subsidized companies. Only Hungary did not agree to the contents of the report. China has been involved in infrastructure projects in central Europe such as the Hungary-Serbia high-speed railway. Although Hungary allowed China to start the project, the EU stopped it, because Budapest allegedly did not publish a call for public tenders and instead relied on bilateral agreements with China. This also shows the political concern of Brussels and the European business sector.

Another problem created by the EU is that it does not trust state-owned enterprises, which of course occupy a large portion of China's foreign investment within the BRI, and everything possible is being done to prevent China's involvement. Of course this EU policy is highly hypocritical if we take into consideration that Greece was obliged to privatize its airports by selling them to the German state-owned FRAPORT. One wonders today what the definition of "privatization" is. European protectionism is increasing while Chinese companies are not yet fully prepared to obey the complicated regulations of the EU. If the BRI is to succeed, a closer bilateral cooperation between the EU and China is needed, so Europe once again becomes the destination of the Silk Road.

It has been said that a potential risk for the BRI would be the eventual disintegration of the EU, since EU funds would no longer be available. I would say the exact opposite: that the eventual dissolution of the EU would actually be a blessing.

Funds would be found on a bilateral basis with European countries and the strict EU rules would no longer exist to hinder investments in European countries by state-owned companies. Furthermore, sanctions of the EU on Russia and China will cease, thus making bilateral cooperation between the European countries with Russia and China more effective. For example, the Russian countermeasures against the EU do not allow agricultural products from Poland to be delivered to China by the China Railway Express through the Eurasian Land-Bridge. Regardless, if the sanctions remain, the construction of the BRI might have to face the risks of poor connectivity. However, after the last G-7 meeting, which isolated the U.S.A., the EU might take a slightly more open attitude towards the BRI, within the framework of its reactions to the tariff war started by Washington.

The United States, India and the BRI

The position of the United States is important as far as BRI is concerned. For the moment, the U.S. position is negatively ambiguous, particularly after it withdrew last year from the Trans-Pacific Partnership trade agreement. It is, however, supporting and participating in the Asia-Africa Growth Corridor, an initiative instigated by Australia, India and Japan and being (unsuccessfully) presented as an alternative to the BRI. Of course the U.S.A. sees China as an antagonist in the race towards global domination. And as long as it continues on that path it will be against the BRI, in spite of the fact that it has much to gain from it. But, as long as the U.S.A. does not physically undermine the project, it is all right. It might even strengthen the cooperation between the participating countries, as a reaction to the U.S. position. India is negative toward the BRI because of the territorial issue that it has with Pakistan concerning Kashmir. India calls the BRI an act of Chinese colonialism. The China-Pakistan Economic Corridor goes through Pakistani occupied Kashmir. India, however, is promoting the India-Myanmar-Thailand highway project (3,200 km) that will link India to the ASEAN countries.

As I mentioned at the outset, economic benefits from a project may overcome political hesitations on conflict-solving. We had two cases of positive outcomes when dealing with the projected route of the Black Sea Ring Highway, a 7,500 km highway that would unite the members of Black Sea Economic Cooperation organization and would facilitate road transport from the Black Sea countries to Europe and Asia.

Problems Overcome

One issue was in Moldova, where the highway was to pass from the self-proclaimed Republic of Transnistria, following the old Soviet highway. The Moldovan authorities were reluctant to have the highway pass through Terespol. At that time, negotiations were being held between the two sides for a possible rapprochement, and the stumbling block was the issue of the identity cards of Terespol. So we told Kisinau to tell the other side that if they accept the Moldovan identity cards and other issues, then the highway would pass through, which is what happened.

The other issue was between Russia and Georgia. The highway was to enter Georgia through Abkhazia, but after the August 2008 war between Russia and Georgia, the latter refused to allow the highway to enter Georgia through Abkhazia. After presenting to the Georgian side in detail the economic benefits that it would have from allowing the highway to go through its territory from Russia, we were finally able to convince Tbilisi to allow the highway to enter through the Roki Tunnel in South Ossetia. The negative position of the United States is the most important element that could hinder progress of the BRI. Bilateral, multilateral or other types of efforts should be undertaken by the participants in order to convince Washington of the benefits that it would have by participating in this project. It is almost a "mission impossible," but at least it should be attempted on a permanent basis, in order to avoid physical hindrance of the BRI. In this sense, closer contacts with Japan, Australia, and India are in order, to examine how the Asia-Africa Growth Corridor could be incorporated within the BRI project. With the EU, there is nothing much that can be done at the present but follow EU rules concerning tenders and financing of projects, so that EU funds can be used by the Central and East European States to partially finance their infrastructure projects.

Culture, Philosophy, Humanism, Spirituality

In a world in which armed conflicts and violence are prevailing and international law has ceased to exist, it is important to stress the role of culture, philosophy, humanism, and spirituality. These intangibles must also be transported through the Silk Road in the form of exchange of ideas and culture between the East and the West. The Schiller Institute, through the active participation of Helga LaRouche in many international fora, is playing a very positive role in this respect. It is in this sense also that Greece held in April of 2017 the first meeting of the Ancient Civilizations Forum with China participating. Follow-up meetings have been held. In conclusion, the successful implementation of the BRI can play an instrumental role in the humanization of international relations, in the economic and cultural development of the people of the participant states, and, in this way, create the conditions for global peace. It might sound like Utopia. But if we do not believe in Utopia, then it will never happen.

SELECTED DISCUSSION AFTER PANEL IV

Uniting Europe on a Higher Level: Italy, Greece, Germany and the European Union

This is an edited transcript of discussion among Claudio Celani, Folker Hellmeyer, Leonidas Chrysanthopoulos, and Helga Zepp-LaRouche, which followed the presentations of Panel IV of the Schiller Institute Conference, on July 1, 2018.

Claudio Celani: I have a question and some comments for Mr. Hellmeyer, concerning his presentation today. As I said yesterday, I admired your recent interview, Mr. Hellmeyer, in which you spoke about Italy and addressed correctly, as do very few people in Germany, the issue of debt, saying, when we consider debt, we have to look at overall debt—public debt and private debt. Looking at this aggregate figure, the problem becomes different, Italy as at the average or even below average level of debt. But where I cannot follow you, is the other part, the part of the structural reforms, the *Aufgaben* [Tasks], in what you said today.

It's a pity that Mr. Zanni, [Member of the European Parliament (MEP) from Italy] is not here—he had to catch a flight. I will try to be an advocate, not for him, but for his reasons, being myself an Italian, who has lived for many decades in Germany, and being a member of the Schiller Institute, I look forward to a well-reasoned argument.

Mr. Zanni showed in his presentation on Panel III that there has been a political response in Italy, as in other countries, to the simple fact that these structural reforms don't work, have not worked: They have not worked in Greece, they have not worked in Italy, but they have not worked in Germany, either. If we look at Germany, what happened with the structural reforms, cost-cutting, and labor reforms? Where are the capital investments in Germany? Where are the investments in infrastructure? You would agree with me that there was a collapse of investment in infrastructure, in capital formation, in all countries in the Eurozone, because of this policy of cutting costs.

Now, concerning Italy—Italy accepted and implemented the *Aufgaben*, since the start of the convergence period in order to join the euro. So, these policies began in 1992. Italy has experienced the greatest level privatization in the West; Italy drastically cut its budget. I think in budget discipline, Italy ranks first in Europe, having reduced the deficit below 3%, constantly, along with other measures. Italy has a primary surplus—it carried out the *Aufgaben*.

The last measures were pension reform and labor reform. And what was labor reform? Labor reform has now made it possible to fake statistics. Today, a person who works only one hour a week, is counted as "employed." So that's how, during the Renzi government, Italy showed a growth of employment, of jobs. The real result, however is that poverty has increased. Poverty has increased throughout Europe, and dramatically in Italy. The latest figures from two days ago: Absolute poverty in Southern Italy is over 10%! Now, these are third world figures, right?

We could go on and on with this discussion, which would be a really nice discussion, were it not for the fact that at the end of the day either my view is implemented or yours is, because we are in this structure of the European Union. And that's a problem.

What I suggest is, to see in what Mr. Zanni said today, the positive aspect, the type of proposal he is putting forward. Mr. Zanni is a younger man, who has come here to speak as a member of the Lega. If you read German media, what is the Lega? "*Rechtsextremist!*" [right-wing extremist] He didn't sound like a *Rechtsextremist*. I know him personally, and he's been my friend for a couple of years. He was elected with the Five Star movement, but then when he saw that the Five Star movement was pushing a neo-liberal agenda in the European Parliament, he decided he had to break with them. He found the Lega, which told him, "You can come with us, you can say whatever you want, and have freedom of expression." He joined the Lega only for that reason.

So, but anyway, his propositional aspect is the China part: let's join to apply the model that China applies in Africa. The European Union should do this, and this is the solution to immigration.

So what's wrong with saying, "Maybe let's reflect on whether integration went too far in Europe? If we go on like this, either we will wind up suppressing elections, or we will have a backlash. Perhaps we will find ourselves having very nasty political forces taking over." So, that's what I think he said, and I think it's a plain proposition. What happens if we take a step back in the monetary integration, in the political integration, but we make a jump forward in physical integration, in investment, and growth?

Folker Hellmeyer: Actually I do not mind investment. What I do mind is consumption. What Italy still needs, and also Greece, are reforms in certain areas in the efficiency of the government, in the political standard, and in the labor market.

The point I want to make is, Italy used to devalue, for instance, like Greece used to devalue in former times. *That is nonstructural.* If you devalue, you have high inflation; if you have high inflation you don't get capital formation, capital investment, because the risk of high inflation is eating up the value of the—thus you betray the young generation of their future. The neglect of political reforms is the prerequisite for the youth problems in the labor market in most of the southern regions. And what we are seeing now is, yes! In order to have the reform, if you implement the reforms, you cut into cold flesh—which is nonproductive of an economy, which is painful. You have high unemployment. But after that, you have a better allocation of all production factors, and then you have sustainable growth again. *Any other issue* is betraying yourself!

We need to do something about deficits. You're right about the net borrowing position of Italy, it is better than Germany, when you look at private households plus government debt. But that's not the point. The point is, to achieve a sustainable, official budget. Otherwise markets will *punish* you! Without the solidarity of Europe, Italy would have gone bankrupt in 2012. It took the "whatever it takes approach" of Mario Draghi, and you know that very well. And *that* is betraying your country!

In the end, we need to stick to certain rules—that's the gold standard—we were all forced to stick to rules. We had lots of nectar, of the new system, where we could run budget deficits like hell. What you did in Italy and what Greece did wrong after getting the euro and a lower interest rate, was consuming it away, you didn't invest it.

I'm very much in favor of investment. On infrastructure, I don't mind running debts on capital investment. I agree with you there.

But we all need to understand that the European family stood together in this crisis, and without our having stood together, there would have been a recession like 1929-32, not only Europe, but for the rest of the world, because of the interconnectedness. That's what we should understand also.

And there's one more issue I want to take up, and this is a really strong mark: After the crisis of 2008-09, the U.S. and the U.K. have repeated the business model that generated the crisis: It's all debt! It's the highest consumer debt, it's the highest corporate debt, and they run a 2.5% growth model with budget deficits of 5.3% this year of GDP, if you rely on the IMF [statistics]. The Eurozone stands at 0.6% this year—IMF numbers—budget deficits with more than 2% growth, and it's recurring income, not credit, which is driving this growth, and *this is good*, and this is structural policy, this is reform policy, this is Aristotle, this is future! Thank you.

Leonidas Chrysanthopoulos: I would like to reply that I totally disagree with you, Mr. Hellmeyer, as far as Greece is concerned. I mean, we had an eight-year program of reforms that destroyed the country! You cannot kill a country, in order to have some GNP and all that. So many people have died! We had human losses, in this thing. The economy has been destroyed. Nothing works in Greece any more, and this is presented as a success.

Plus—and this is something else that you don't know about, of course: We have another problem, another issue, which is the German debt to Greece on the loan that Germany took during the Greek occupation [1941-1944], which is worth, today,— it's value is much bigger than the Greek debt. But that's another story. That concerns the Greek governments, the quisling governments, who refused to raise the issue with Germany, and who still do refuse that.

But we started the reform program, the aim of which was to diminish Greece's debt, which in 2010 was 120% of the GDP. Today it's 185%. So, it's eight years of failure! And there's nobody in the EU willing to take responsibility for this failure. Even the IMF has said that it failed, but the politicians refuse to change that policy, because they refuse to admit that they made a mistake. I cannot, and many Greeks can no longer tolerate to see their country being destroyed like that, by the EU! Of which we are members.

I won't continue. Thank you.

Zepp-LaRouche: I would like to point to the fact that there is a reason why the EU is in the condition it is. When the East European countries, the 16+1 and Greece and Serbia and other countries wanted to be part of the Belt and Road Initiative, there was a violent reaction from Brussels, and also from the former German Economics Minister, Sigmar Gabriel, who said that China is destroying the European Union and causing disunity. And then the Chinese answered, the EU does not need China to be disunited, they're disunited all by themselves. The offer of the Chinese Belt and Road Initiative is the only way to unite Europe on a higher level.

And that is, I think, something we should look at.

Look, there are many problems which are self-evident: One is Africa. Africa is in the condition it is in, not because of China, but because of the West! The West did not develop Africa, neither in the colonial times, nor in the time of the IMF conditionalities, and part of the reason why the refugee crisis exists is because of the policy of the EU and the IMF and World Bank, which up to this present day are not making the kind of investment in Africa which would alleviate the problem.

As a matter fact, we have many contacts, Mittelstand people, who tell us they would like to invest in Africa, but for the German government, and the EU. The German government hides behind the EU, saying they wouldn't get the kind of [investment protection] umbrella which they would need, because, as Herr von Helldorff was saying, the big DAX firms are not the problem, the problem is the SMEs [small and medium-size enterprises] who need the protection of the state and treaties among the states to be able, otherwise the risk is too big for them.

So look at Africa as a result of this policy. Look at the condition of the Southern European countries, Portugal, Spain. Portugal is doing a little bit better now, but Spain, Greece, Italy. I mean, the suicide rates, the increase in the death rate, the collapse of the birth rate, these are all factors of—I hate to say it—[Germany's former Finance Minister] Mr. Schäuble's "black zero" [no deficit policy]. And Schäuble was the one who was a leading person to impose the kind of austerity policy, and it did not work!

And I think we should rather have a future orientation. The good thing is that we agree that the solution is the Silk Road.

I am open to the EU reforming itself. However, I have no reason at this point to believe that this will happen; but if they do, so be it, its fine with me. I'm not dogmatic on this point, but the change has to occur. I think that protecting the German capital stock and the hidden champions and all of this, does not require a supranational structure which is completely alienated from its own people. You could have the same kind of protection with a de Gaulle type of alliance of sovereign nation-states who work together for a joint mission.

We are working to bring about a New Paradigm, which is very much in cohesion with what Xi Jinping is saying about a new international relationship among nations based on respect for sovereignty, equality, and non-interference. If that principle would also be part of a Eurasian union from Vladivostok to Lisbon, I think it would work perfectly fine. We need new principles in international politics, because staying with the geopolitical view will not function. We need a new international set of relations, based on these ideas.

You're Human!
Do You Know What That Means?

by Robert Ingraham

PART THREE OF A SERIES
The necessity for the human mind to create that which is new will be the topic in this third part of our series.

III.
The Power of Discovery

July 3—First, let us dispense with the lying frauds that have been handed down to us by that carnival barker for the British Empire, Charles Darwin, to wit, that mankind's evolution stemmed from "natural selection" and "survival of the fittest."

To simplify, the argument goes something like this: As the human species progressed, it adapted. It had an apposable thumb; it possessed a larger cranial size; it went through mutations and change in DNA make-up—all of which can be measured and analyzed mathematically. Over time, through trial and error, mankind developed (stumbled upon) new types of tools and ways of using them. Somehow, in some way, the human species progressed, as sort of a "smart monkey."

Edgar Alan Poe would laugh at such an analysis. The secret to

A cartoon caricature depicting Charles Darwin as the original smart monkey.

the Promethean emergence of the human species is hidden in plain sight. Every leap forward, each intervention that unlocked new potentials for upward human development, flowed from an act of Discovery, from a

power that exists in the minds of human beings and is nowhere else to be found—as a self-conscious deliberate force—in the biosphere.

As stated earlier, any competent investigation must begin with the axiom-shattering implication of the human species' mastery and deployment of the power of fire. This is where the essence—the being—of the human identity is to be found: the discovery of new universal principles which enhance mankind's power over nature and increase the population and productivity of the human species. None of the stunning breakthroughs accomplished by individual humans can be explained by the image of a Paleolithic brute scratching around in the dirt and learning through "sense-experience."

Communicating Ideas

In his 1998 essay "When Economics Becomes Science," Lyndon LaRouche addresses directly the source from which all human progress flows. One short excerpt indicates LaRouche's approach:

The characteristic—characteristically anti-entropic quality— of non-linear action, of any viable economic process, is the anti-entropic action located within the interval defined by a single individual's generation, of a single, validated new principle of our universe. It is the efficient relationship between that individual's sovereign cognitive action, and the increased power of the entire society in the universe, which is the essential definition of the science of physical economy. The kernel of that characteristic, determining relationship, is expressed in that Riemannian form of multiply-connected manifold, "n+m," we have identified above.

These sentences by Lyndon LaRouche provide the

only legitimate starting point for beginning an investigation into the truth about human advancement. For the remainder of this part of our discussion, we shall look at several human discoveries, including astronomy, navigation, and chemistry. We will preface those remarks with a look at how early Man sought to express the thoughts of his own mind. In all of this, what must be kept foremost is the appreciation of the anti-entropic power of the individual human mind in discovering new universal principles, which in LaRouche's words, led to an "increased power of the entire society in the universe."

There is a great deal of guess-work—and that's what it is—about when the human species first developed the use of language. The work in this field is poisoned by those who demand that human evolution must be examined *biologically*, not *cognitively*. In truth, the phenomenon of individual human discovery and the *socialization of discovery* are inseparable. The individual human being is both a creative, as well as a social individual, and it is self-evident that the communication of ideas has been part of human existence, even going back as far as the discovery of the use of fire. Only irrationalists or British oligarchs would deny this.

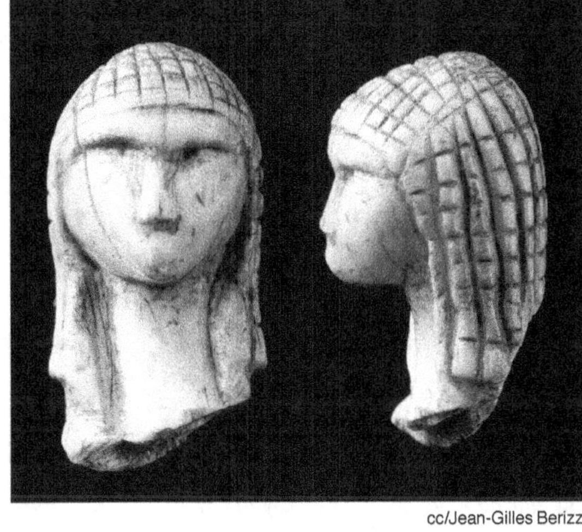

cc/Jean-Gilles Berizzi

Front and side views of the Venus of Brassempouy, one of the earliest known realistic representations of the human face.

Concepts are formed and articulated with one's own power of imagination. An hypothesis is tested. A validated discovery is confirmed. Then, the social man acts to communicate his discovery and the *process of discovery itself* to his brethren. Such defines human social development. The human mind is more powerful—as a universal force—than any physical process, and the discovery of new universal principles and the socialization of those principles is the only legitimate definition of human culture. In studying the history of the human race, it is this cognitive footprint which the professional investigator must seek out.

All of the pre-historic physical evidence which has survived to the present day merely represents the *products* of acts of human discovery. What is more difficult—much more difficult—is to delve into the question of pre-historic human *noëtics* itself, and the further back one goes, the archeological record which will hint at the tell-tale signs becomes thinner and thinner.

Despite these difficulties, what has been un-covered to date is a revelation. Cave paintings still exist which are 40,000 years old; carved figures and statues exist from about the same period, and the earliest musical instruments go back to at least 30,000 BC, as does pottery. The oldest known engraved figures, dating to 70,000 BC, were recently discovered at the Blombos Cave, near Cape Town, South Africa. Numerous sites from Africa, to Europe, to China, to Indonesia, to Australia and many places in-between have yielded such artifacts. In all of this, we find the Mind of Man—exploring the nature of the universe and biosphere, depicting both physical advances of the human species (Riemann's "n-fold" manifold) and artistic expressions of the human identity (Riemann's "m-fold" manifold).

Look at the ivory statue of the Venus de Brassempouy, dated 26,000 BC. Was this the product of a brutish primitive human mind? Was this created by someone scratching in the dirt?

Human beings of the late-Paleolithic era deployed fire, investigated astronomy, navigated the seas, built dwellings, possessed finely-made tools, pottery, and implements, and they developed a remarkable aesthetic sensibility, as evidenced by the paintings and other works they left behind.

These were all the products of individual human beings, examining the nature of the universe, discovering new physical principles, and communicating these discoveries to fellow human beings.

The Mind and the Universe

The nature of human existence is that the individual is always in an internal dialogue with himself—questioning, investigating and formulating hypotheses. This is where "human nature" is to be found, and Man has always sought means to communicate the products of these deliberations and discoveries among his fellow men. As Lyndon LaRouche states,[1] truthful human communication is based on "prompting the other person

1. Again, in "When Economics Becomes a Science," reprinted in *EIR*, June 1, 2018.

to undergo the same creative process we have experienced within our own minds." This did not begin at some later date. It has been with us since a man—or a woman—lit the first human-controlled fire.

We see the evidence of this human passion to communicate discoveries and to pass them down to future generations in the emergence of what is sometimes called the "oral tradition," e.g., the Epics of Homer, the Fables of Aesop, and many other early works to be found in human settlements from throughout the world. Passed down for centuries—or even longer—usually sung, these renderings provide a picture of Man's continuing investigation into the secrets of the universe. These are not just stories or myths.

Astronomy takes center stage in many of the tales,

cc/José-Manuel Benito

A limestone Kish tablet from Sumer with pictographic writing may be the earliest known writing, dating from 3500 BC.

sometimes directly but often cloaked as metaphors, parables and anthropomorphisms, such as the personification of the Pleiades and other asterisms. The relationship of the human race to the greater celestial heaven, and the influence of the constellations on human existence appear again and again in the form of investigating the lawfulness of celestial motion. Geological processes and the crises which mankind had been forced to overcome also appear, including descriptions of famines and the effects of catastrophic weather changes from the earlier glacial and post-glacial periods. More will be said about all of this, particularly in relation to Homer, below.

As to written language, its origin may never be known. For those humans who lived prior to the last glacial maximum, nothing in the form of written languages—if they existed—survives. What is clear, however, is that the origin of written language preceded, by many millennia, the Mesopotamian Temple Culture of Sumer. Evidence of much earlier writing from Henan Province in China, dated at 6,400 BC, as well as from

several other locations, has been confirmed. One example is the Dispilio tablet, found in Macedonia and dated to 5,300 BC; another is the Vinca script, a set of symbols found on 6th millennium BC artifacts from the Vinca culture of southeastern Europe, an area also known for the early production of copper.

Astronomy

If you study a variety of creatures—cows, cats, sheep, and the like—you will notice that they almost never look up into the sky. Their eyes are directed downward, toward the search for food, possible enemies, or potential mates. Yet, for as long as humans have existed, our vision has been drawn upward. The searching of the heavens for truth, for lawfulness, has

cc/Chris S. Henshilwood

Engraved ochre from Blombos Cave in South Africa.

distinguished humanity from the beginning. These ancient astronomers were not simply "observing patterns in the sky." Individual acts of discovery took place—efforts to coax the universe to disclose its secrets, to unveil the lawful ordering of the celestial environment. As long as Man has existed he has sought to understand—and to bring within the self-conscious body of human culture—the nature of the universe—and his own role in ongoing creation.

In China, evidence of advanced astronomical observation has been found dating back to at least 14,000 BC, well into the period of the last glaciation. Additionally, the evidence presented by Bal Gangadhar Tilak in his *Orion* (1893) and *Arctic Home in the Vedas* (1903) is conclusive as to the pre-Mesopotamian development of a sophisticated study of astronomy.[2] There also exist numerous artifacts and ruins from the Neolithic era which were clearly devoted to astronomical observation. The Goseck

---

2. See: "The Present Scientific Implications of Vedic Calendars from the Standpoint of Kepler and Circles of Gauss," by Lyndon H, LaRouche, Jr.

circle, located in Germany and discovered in 1991, is dated to 5,000 BC. It is currently the oldest known "solar observatory" in the world. And then there are the Egyptian pyramids, which date to at latest 2,600 BC.

In Homer's *Iliad* and *Odyssey* we find an extensive discussion and understanding of astronomical processes. The motions of Sirius, Orion, Ursa Major, Venus, the Pleiades, and many other celestial bodies and asterisms are described and discussed numerous times. One example which Homer presents is that the mid-summer appearance of Sirius above the horizon in the evening sky heralds a season of hot dry weather. Sirius is the brightest star of the constellation Canis Major (Greater Dog), and it is the annual appearance of Sirius which has given us the modern expression "dog days of summer."

In Book 20 of the *Odyssey*, Homer also depicts a solar eclipse. What is most remarkable about this is that Homer also describes the precise position of Venus (high in the sky), the visibility of the Pleiades, and the retrograde motion of Mercury (Hermes) low in the evening sky. Recent astronomical research has shown that the occurrence of a solar eclipse with the precise conjunction of these three other astronomical events actually occurred about 1188 BC, almost 300 years before Homer was born, and approximately at the time of the downfall of Troy.

Navigation

Again, from Homer, the *Odyssey* Book 5:

His sails expos'd, and hoisèd. Off he gat;
And cheerful was he. At the stern he sat,
And steer'd right artfully, nor sleep could seize
His eyelids. He beheld the Pleiades;
The Bear, surnamed the Wain, that round doth move
About Orion, and keeps still above
The billowy ocean; the slow-setting star
Boötes call'd, by some the waggoner.
Calypso warn'd him he his course should steer
Still to his left hand.

　　　　　　　—translated by George Chapman

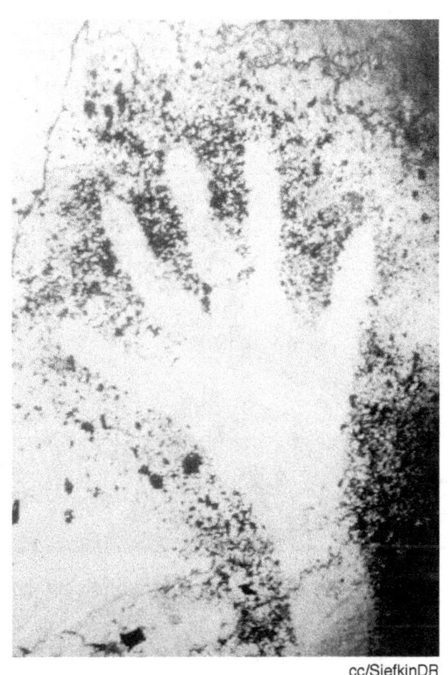

cc/SiefkinDR

Stencil of a human hand from Cosquer cave, near Marseille, France, dating from 27,000 Before Present Era.

This is a description of navigation, over open sea, by the stars. The human species is the only creature capable of this, and this power was only made possible through an advanced understanding of astronomy. Open sea navigation was not accomplished through "trial and error," i.e., get in a raft and hope for the best. The voyages of exploration which were carried out, as well as human emigration to distant lands, were all conducted by a human culture based on a growing body of scientific knowledge.

Evidence exists that humans were traveling over open bodies of water as early as 800,000 BC. After 100,000 BC, when *Homo sapiens* began to move out of Africa in large numbers, it is certain that this involved crossing the Red Sea in boats. There is also the case of Australia, where archaeological findings have dated the arrival of humans to no later than 40,000 BC, at a time—as today—when Australia was surrounded by water and could only be reached by voyage over open ocean.

Evidence exists of a late-Paleolithic maritime human culture, although most of the physical remains have been lost. During the last glacial maximum, the level of the oceans, worldwide, was about 400 feet lower than at present. Take a look at depth charts. Along many current shorelines, to reach a water depth of 400 feet you have to go several miles—or more—off shore. The centuries before the last glacial melt were the era of human expansion to every continent in the world (with the exception of Antarctica), and all of the coastal communities and villages that existed during those crucial centuries are long-ago submerged, covered with water, silt, sand, debris, and vegetation.

Take the case of the now famous Cosquers Grotto, off the coast of southern France, near Marseilles. In 1985, the entranceway to the Grotto was accidentally discovered by a French diver 121 feet below the surface. You can only access the grotto by swimming underwater through a long tunnel. Much of the contents of the Grotto have been destroyed by seawater, but at least 150 cave paintings still exist, some dating back to at latest 25,000 BC, at a time when the entire cave would have been on solid ground.

There is also the evidence from the Gulf of Cambay, off the coast of western India, where fossils dated to 7,500 BC have been recovered from a depth of 120 feet; or the underwater structures near Yonaguni, off the coast of Japan, dated to 8,000 BC. Similar findings have been reported from Mexico, to Morocco, to Scotland and South America.

The truth is inescapable. Mankind is a sea-faring species, and exploration and emigration over open seas is interwoven with a growing mastery of the understanding of astronomical processes, the motion of the stars, the sun and moon, as well as a deepening knowledge of ocean currents and weather patterns.

Chemistry

During the "Stone Age," human beings did not simply find rocks lying around on the ground and break them into pieces which could be used as "tools." Flint, for example, is a form of the mineral quartz. It occurs chiefly as nodules and masses in sedimentary rocks, such as chalks and limestones. It has to be located, identified, dug out of the ground, and then chiseled to create any tools worth using. It is clear that the origin of this form of organized "mining" is far back in the Paleolithic, more than a million years ago.

The great discovery came when the extraction of raw materials was combined with fire, resulting in the invention of pottery, i.e., the chemical transformation of a raw material to a new manmade state from which it could not revert to its natural form. This discovery is precisely what Lyndon LaRouche means when he discusses how a single act of individual human discovery produces an anti-entropic leap in the power of the human species—an action which defines a new manifold of human potentiality.

Currently, the earliest date given for the application of fire to create new materials is about 30,000 BC, but as with all of these dates, nothing is certain. What is known is that it was not long before the fire-driven processes were applied to working with metals, as well as to the invention of new metals, i.e., substances which had no prior existence.

Much of this progress, including the usage of copper, iron and bronze, as well as the beginnings of animal domestication, was centered in a region which stretches from the Caspian Sea, through the Caucasus,[3] along the shore of the Black Sea, into northern Anatolia, and then ending in the Balkans. The use of copper in tool-making dates back to at latest 9,000 BC, probably earlier, and the earliest verifiable high-temperature "copper-works" are from an archaeological site in present-day Serbia. The earliest large-scale smelting of iron took place in Eastern Anatolia, and the earliest known surviving iron artifacts were discovered in northern Iran. Glass was also invented in the same region.

Many of these developments were made possible by the invention of charcoal. Unshakable evidence exists of the use of charcoal by humans as early as 32,000 BC, and it was the application of charcoal to the production of copper which ushered in modern metallurgy, also making possible the later production of both bronze and iron. Charcoal burns at temperatures up to 2,700 °C. By comparison, the melting point of iron is approximately 1,500 °C. Charcoal made large-scale metal-working feasible.

The invention of bronze supplied humanity with an enormous new power in terms of physical economy. Take a minute to consider what the manufacture of bronze involves. First, the copper has to be extracted from stone ore, which itself requires a high level of creative imagination. The addition of tin to create the *manmade* alloy bronze, a substance which had no prior existence, was the cognitive breakthrough. Working with copper, tin, and bronze involved blast furnaces, welding, soldering and the use of rivets, as well as large-scale engineering. The invention of bronze led to the rapid introduction of new types of tools such as plows, wheels, etc., resulting in a non-linear surge in mankind's productive power.

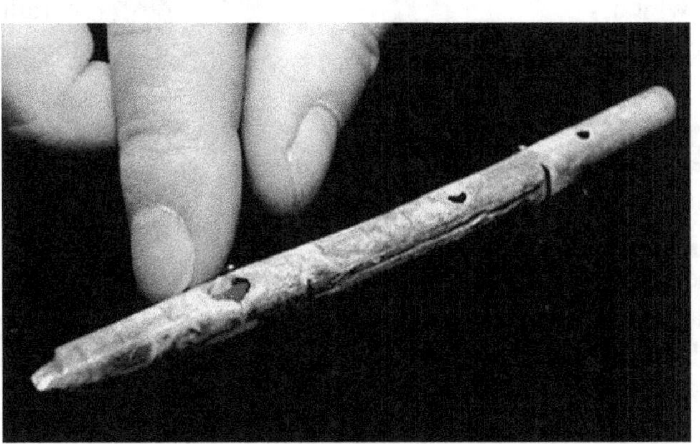

A 35,000 year old flute, an early example of metal working.

---

3. Interestingly, a region associated with Prometheus, the fire-bringer.

Human-Steered Evolution

During the late Paleolithic, mankind began to create a human-directed biosphere. Take the case of animals and plants. A recent discovery along the shore of the Sea of Galilee has proven that human beings were tending plants, including barley and oats, 23,000 years ago. The more important issue, however, is not the date of these developments, but the actual nature of what humans were creating.

Consider the actual mental concept behind the word "domestication." Common-place usage defines the word to be synonymous with the idea that humans simply managed to "tame" wild animals, or discovered how to grow what were then pre-existing wild grains and vegetables. That idea is completely wrong-one hundred percent wrong. One example should suffice:

The grain we call "corn," did not exist 50,000 years ago. Instead, a nearly inedible wild grain known as teosinte was its primitive ancestor. Through centuries of cross-breeding and experimentation, teosinte was transformed—by man—into the usable maize, which after further human intervention, was developed into modern corn. The corn which you enjoy at a Fourth of July picnic bears almost no resemblance to teosinte; it is entirely the product of centuries of human creative intervention. In reality, the human species has invented the food it eats. Humanity does not live off nature.

This same human intervention characterizes human relations with the lower beasts. Sheep and goats appear to have been the first animals (other than dogs)[4] brought into the human-directed economy. All modern sheep are descended from the wild *mouflon*, and goats are descended from the *bezoar goat*. Both creatures inhabited the mountain slopes from central Turkey, eastward into northern Iraq and Iran. As with corn, modern sheep and goats bear little resemblance to their wild ancestors. Ten-thousand-year-old skeletons of these creatures already show significant physical transformations, indicating generations of human-steered breeding methods to develop a more

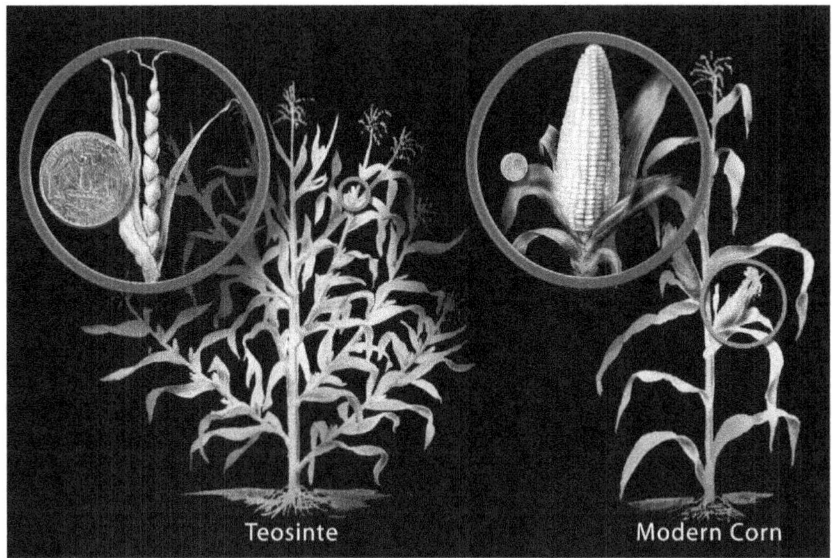

Nicolle Rager Fuller, National Science Foundation

Cultivated corn was domesticated from teosinte more than 6,000 years ago.

productive variation of the individual species.

What we are really dealing with is not "domestication," but new manmade species which were then incorporated into human culture—a human-steered biosphere. This, together with the breakthroughs in astronomy, metallurgy and navigation, produced a new type of human society, more productive, using increasing amounts of energy per-capita, and capable of supporting denser population development.

The life-span increased. Nutrition improved. The development of agriculture was accompanied by new methods of flood control and irrigation, including the construction of canals and dikes. Mining for salt began, which allowed—for the first time—for the large-scale preservation of food. Fermentation was invented to prevent water-borne diseases. Ploughs and wagons were introduced. The use of brick in buildings and foundations, and the grinding of grain into flour became widespread. The engineering of boats improved, and seaborne human colonization became common. Humanity had not only survived the extinction threats of the Paleolithic Era, but firmly established human civilization on every corner of the planet.

This is Vernadsky's Noösphere asserting dominion over the biosphere, and acting to improve and upgrade that biosphere such that it will serve to further increase the potential for new human discoveries. All of this originated in the power of discovery which exists in each sovereign human individual.

To be continued.

---

4. Man's companion, the dog, was domesticated at least 30,000 years ago, and there are even claims of dog fossils found alongside humans from 100,000 BC.

June 2, 1995

The Dynamics of the Global Economic Breakdown

by Lyndon H. LaRouche, Jr.

It is impossible to represent any political-economy competently, unless every existing national economy, and also that of the world as a whole, is understood as a process of dynamic interaction among axiomatically distinct types of political-economic processes, the which are as distinct from one another as the different species which interact within a jungle habitat.[1] The failure of financial authorities and others to comprehend this issue, is key to the fact that governments, as well as leading monetary and financial institutions, in their blindness to this scientific issue, have mis-led the world to the very brink of the greatest economic collapse in modern history.

The corollary of the ontological paradox defined by Plato's **Parmenides,** is that any single element of an array described as a "Many," can exist, both simultane-

ously and efficiently, as a phenomenon of two or more mutually exclusive axiomatic systems. The meaning of that fact is supplied, not by the individual phenomenon as such, but, rather, by the "One" which subsumes the "Many" of which that individual phenomenon is perceived, axiomatically, to be a member.[2]

The manner in which this problem presents itself in the domain of economy, should prompt us to think, comparatively, of the broadly analogous, anomalous relationship in the interaction of non-living and living processes generally. A related topic might be the study of effectively interacting processes on the respectively macroscopic, sub-atomic, and astrophysical scale.

This notion, just stated, is the required, rigorous approach to correction of the prevalent, worldwide occurrence of *fallacy of composition* in today's economic analysis and forecasting.[3]

---

1. The model of reference for our employment of the term "axiomatic," here, and throughout this report, is formal (i.e., deductive) Euclidean geometry. All of the allowed propositions of such a system aform a deductive lattice-work of theorems (e.g., a "theorem-lattice"), provided each is not inconsistent with any among the set of axioms and postulates underlying each and all theorems of that lattice. That set of underlying, axiomatic assumptions represents, thus, what Plato defines as a *species* of deductive system. The Euclidean type is also one of the lower forms of what Plato defines as an *hypothesis.* "Hypothesis" also signifies a fundamental discovery in science: i.e., the replacement of one set of axioms by another set—a new hypothesis, defining thus an absolute formal discontinuity between the first axiomatic system (theorem-lattice) and its successor. As Bernhard Riemann emphasized in his "*Die Unterscheidung, welche Newton zwischen Bewegungsgesetzen oder Axiomen under Hypothesen macht, scheint mir nicht haltbar....*" **Werke** (New York: Dover Publications, Inc., 1953), p.525: Newton spoke falsely when he wrote "*hypotheses non fingo;*" his entire system rests upon hypothetical assumptions, either copied from Sarpi-Galileo, or arbitrarily supplied by himself. As Riemann notes, at least one axiom within Newton's system, respecting motion and inertia, is untenable.

2. Plato, **Parmenides,** in **Plato: Cratylus, Parmenides, Greater Hippias, Lesser Hippias,** trans. by H.N. Fowler, Loeb Classical Library (Cambridge: Harvard University Press, 1926).

3. The famous example of "fallacy of composition" is "man is a featherless biped." For example: fallacy of composition is a principal means used by politically motivated Federal and state prosecutions in bringing about, fraudulently, criminal conviction of innocent defendants. For example: In **U.S.A. vs. LaRouche, et al., 1988 (Eastern District of Virginia: Cr. No. 88-00243-A),** in addition to the prosecutors' heavy reliance upon their own lying and subornation of perjury, the most notable trick employed to achieve fallacy of composition was a fraudulent *in limine* ruling, which suppressed precisely that evidence which would have shown that it was the prosecution, rather than the defendants, which had perpetrated each and all of the offenses with which the defendants were charged. Relative to the fraudulent "man is a featherless biped": Man is the only creature which has the manifest ability to change willfully its own characteristic behavior as a species: Any definition of man which does not include the facts bearing upon that uniqueness of our species, is a fallacy of composition.

The blindness of the financial "authorities" to the issues of scientific method has brought the world to the brink of economic collapse. Shown here are participants in a Jan. 5, 1995 hearing of the Senate Banking, Housing, and Urban Affairs Committee, on the issue of financial derivatives. Left to right: Mary Schapiro, chairman of the Commodity Futures Trading Commission; Arthur Levitt, chairman of the Securities and Exchange Commission; Federal Reserve Board Chairman Alan Greenspan; Sen. Alphonse D'Amato (R-N.Y.), chairman of the committee.

Significantly, according to this rule of scientific method, any event in the U.S. economy today, is both an individual phenomenon within the axiomatic domain of the monetary system, and, simultaneously, in that physical-economic process which lies axiomatically, outside the monetary process's theorem-lattice.

The most effective way in which to address the complications which arise from such coincidences, is to begin from the standpoint of the relevant, conflicting axiomatics. In this approach, before examining the statistical arrays presented, one must first define the process as an interaction among the relevant, mutually exclusive axiomatic systems represented. Only after that task has been completed, should the statistical array be analyzed.

Summary Review: Axiomatics of Political-Economy

Begin our consideration of interaction of axiomatically mutually exclusive systems, with a summary review of the mutually exclusive species of modern political-economic doctrine and practice.

What is known as "modern political economy," grew out of the A.D. 1461 accession of France's King Louis XI to become the founder of the first modern, sovereign nation-state. The reforms in statecraft pioneered under Louis XI, revolutionized human existence, producing a new form of society, which had never existed prior to Europe's Fifteenth Century. The emergence of this new form of national economy, based on state ordering of generalized technological progress, led to the emergence of modern European civilization as the dominant political force on this planet. All subsequently influential currents of thought on modern political-economy, whether cohering with, or opposed to Louis XI's reforms, were obliged to address that phenomenon of "macro-economic profit," the which is a distinguishing characteristic of the durable form of all modern national economies.

The principal doctrines of modern political-economy are divided, axiomatically, among five influential "species." These "species" are assorted, in turn, between two "families." These may be represented summarily, as follows.

Family #1: Cameralism. From the time of the accession of France's Louis XI, and the introduction of his new, "commonwealth" form of modern nation-state, the emphasis of the modern statecraft following in his footsteps, was the increase of the well-being and productivity of the individual and family household, per capita of labor-force, per household, and per unit of land-area utilized. The spectacular success of France's national economy under Louis XI's "commonwealth" policies, is exemplary. This view of required political-economic practice, was a characteristic feature of a branch of studies in statecraft known as "cameralism."

During the most recent three centuries, there has been but one "species" of this axiomatic "family." That species emerged during the late Seventeenth Century, as the impact of Leibniz's revolutionary application of his principles of a science of physical economy to the cameralist statecraft of France's great minister, Jean-Baptiste Colbert. The characteristic outgrowth of the combined influence of Colbert and Leibniz, is known as the *"American System of political-economy,"* as associated with such names as U.S. Treasury Secretary Alexander Hamilton, Mathew Carey, and Friedrich List.

This axiomatic "species" of political-economy is best represented by aid of this writer's own original discoveries, dating from work of the 1948-52 interval; this resulted in a more advanced version of Leibniz's original *science of physical economy.*[4]

Using a modern classroom's language, the elements of consumption of *those* specific qualities of physical goods and services which are functionally essential for maintaining the current rate of "macroeconomic" profit-potential, may be described as "the energy of the system" of that political economy taken as a whole. The increase of the output of those specific qualities of goods and services, in excess of the currently estimable "energy of the system," represents what the ordinary classroom today would identify conveniently as the "free energy" of the productive process. Hence, "rate of profit" (per capita, per household, per unit of land-area used) is typified descriptively as the ratio of the "free energy" to the "energy of the system."

As to functionally essential qualities of physical goods consumed, these include the following general types. 1) Physical goods: a) Basic economic infrastructure; b) Agricultural and mining goods; c) Manufacturing goods; d) Physical goods of forms of production other than infrastructure, agriculture, mining, and manufacturing, such as construction. 2) Services, or "soft" forms of basic economic infrastructure: a) Classical-humanist forms of content of primary and secondary education, and Classical-humanist forms of higher education (excluding positivist pseudo-sciences such as sociology, anthropology, behaviorist psychology, and "political science"); b) Scientific and technological progress as such; c) Those aspects of health-care which are essential to maintaining and improving the demographic characteristics of health and longevity of the population and its households.[5]

Other categories of services, to the degree they are essential to the functioning of the modern form of nation-state, are treated as "general overhead," and are properly limited in relative quantity by a strict sense of how much of this should be allowed, as distinct from excessive growth of sales, bureaucratic, and non-essential "service" functions in the private and public sectors.

The key to maintenance and growth of the scale and rate of profit is energy-intensive, capital-intensive modes of investment in scientific, technological, and related cultural progress. The correlative of this, from the time of France's Louis XI, is the introduction of the Classical-humanist methods of secondary education as the basis for bringing children and adolescents, including orphans and offspring of economically poor households, into a secondary-educational program which tends to foster the production of geniuses.

One may sum up the result: The source of the not-entropic growth of a successful form of modern nation-state's political economy, is the nurture and expression of that creative potential of the individual person which otherwise sets the human species axiomatically apart from, and above all other species.

Family #2: "Profit" as a Metaphysical Secretion of an Epiphenomenalist Principle of Formal Logic. The first influential attempts at a theory of political-economy contrary to the cameralist practice of Louis XI,

---

4. See Lyndon H. LaRouche, Jr., "On LaRouche's Discovery," **Fidelio**, Spring 1994. On the application of that discovery to political-economy, see his introductory textbook, **So, You Wish to Learn All About Economics?** (New York: New Benjamin Franklin House, 1984) Kindle or EPUB, and his **The Science of Christian Economy** (Washington, D.C.: Schiller Institute, 1991).

5. The relevant measurements consider not only the ratio of "free energy" to "energy of the system." The level of "energy of the system," per capita (of potential labor-force), per family household, and per unit of land-area employed (e.g., per square kilometer), must be taken into account. The power, usable-water throughput, and ton-miles/hour of freight (all considered per capita, per household, and per unit of land-area), which correspond to that level of technology, must also be considered. It is man's willful change in society's relationship to nature, which is the subject of our measure of effective productivity.

Colbert, and Leibniz, emerged beginning the early Eighteenth Century. Each of the "species" of political-economy of this axiomatic family-type, is commonly characterized by the attempt to explain the appearance of "macroeconomic" profit according to the notion of *epiphenomena* outlined in Aristotle's frankly hysterical **Metaphysics.**

Until the appearance of the *systems analysis* dogma of John Von Neumann, during the late 1930s, there were but three notable "species" of this family. In order of their appearance, they are: a) the pro-feudalist *Physiocratic* dogma of France's Dr. François Quesnay, b) the pro-financier-nobility dogma of the British East India Company's Haileybury school, typified by Adam Smith's **Wealth of Nations,** and c) the dogma which Karl Marx's **Capital** derived from an axiomatic change in the dogmas of both the Physiocratic and Haileybury schools of political-economy.

The additional, fourth species of this same family emerged during the most recent several decades. The axiomatic innovations in the Haileybury school introduced by John Von Neumann ("systems analysis") and Prof. Norbert Wiener ("information theory"), have become the political-economic dogma of the "Third Wave" cult, as typified by Britain's Lord William Rees-Mogg, Alvin Toffler, and U.S. Speaker of the House of Representatives Newt(on) Gingrich.

Quesnay, a French asset of the Venice intelligence service, and an ideological spokesman for France's neo-feudal, chronically treasonous, anglophile *Fronde* tradition, insisted that profit is an epiphenomenon of the "Bounty of Nature," which is asserted to be God's gift to that class of feudal landowners to whom God has given their property-title. Smith copies—virtually plagiarizes—the French Physiocrats Quesnay and Turgot, for the most part; he copies blindly and faithfully, Quesnay's feudal dogma of *laissez-faire* as "free trade;" but, he changes the axiomatic definition of the source of the epiphenomenon of profit, from the feudalist's "Bounty of Nature," to the London, Venice-modelled, financier-nobility's tribute from the "Bounty of Trade." Karl Marx shifts the epiphenomenon axiomatically, to the labor of the proletariat; Frederick Engels goes so far as to attribute technology to epiphenomena of the mechanics of the opposable thumb. The contemporary followers of Von Neumann and Wiener, such as Toffler, Rees-Mogg, and Gingrich, shift the axiomatically attributed source of profit, axiomatically, to the epiphenomena of modern mechanistic gas-theory, Wiener's gas-theory-based dogma of "information."

Within each of the two, mutually exclusive "families" of modern political-economy, each species is distinguished from the others by some included difference in axiom. The respective "families" are distinguished from one another by a difference in method of defining the axiomatic principles underlying a theorem-lattice. In Plato's method, for example, the set of axioms which underlies any species of theorem-lattice, would be identified as an *hypothesis*; the difference in method which renders "families" of such "species" mutually exclusive, would be identified as a matter of *higher hypothesis.*

The interaction of individual phenomena common to systems of mutually exclusive axiomatic quality, must be viewed in this light. The key to mastering that challenge in terms such as those of modern mathematical physics, is implicitly provided in Bernhard Riemann's 1854 habilitation dissertation, "On The Hypotheses Which Underlie Geometry."[6]

The British Versus U.S.A. System

The simultaneous increase of a society's per-capita "energy of the system," and also a persistence, or even a rise in the ratio of "free energy" to "energy of the system," is a clear "violation" of what are loosely described as the three "Laws" of Clausius-Kelvin thermodynamics. This aspect of modern European civilization is but a more conspicuous expression of the historical fact, of the not-entropic rise of mankind's potential relative population-density, in a manner impossible among inferior species. That is a crucial fact of the matter which must be addressed, as a precondition for any competent examination of modern systems and doctrines of political-economy.

The academically formal difficulties thus presented are more readily overcome by a reference to the Nineteenth-Century origins of modern, positivist versions of taught thermodynamics. The manner in which Clausius, Grassmann, and Kelvin concocted this mechanistic interpretation of Sadi Carnot's work, is aptly indicated by their fellow-ideologue James C. Maxwell.

---

6. *Über die Hypothesen, welche der Geometrie zu Grunde liegen,* **Bernhard Riemann's Gesammelte Mathematische Werke** (New York: Dover Publications, Inc. [reprint of original Tübner 1902 edition], 1953), pp. 272-287. Riemann should be read in his own, Platonic terms, disregarding the "spin-doctored" commentaries of authorities antagonistic to Riemann's principle, from the pro-Hegel Prof. Felix Klein, on down.

Maxwell was chided for using, unacknowledged, the discoveries of such predecessors as Wilhelm Weber and Bernhard Riemann. To this, he replied in a letter, that he had suppressed the fact of his plagiarism, which he considered justified by his faction's refusal to recognize the existence of any physical geometries "but our own." The arbitrary claim of "universal entropy" arose during the Nineteenth Century, in the manner indicated by Maxwell's response. *That claim rests absolutely upon the validity of an arbitrary, axiomatic assumption imposed upon the mathematics employed by Clausius, Grassmann, Kelvin, Helmholtz, Maxwell, et al., in arbitrary* counterposition to the greatest mathematicians and physicists of that century, such as Gauss, Weber, and Riemann.

Clausius and Kelvin placed themselves in an absurd position, by arguing, implicitly, that their opinion is the epiphenomenon of a "not-entropic" process, human existence, a process which that opinion decrees could not possibly exist.[7]

As long as we remain distant from those extremes of scale called microphysics and astrophysics, we remain in a (macro-scale) domain which either belongs to phenomena attributable to the senses, or nearly so. In this middle range of observation and ontological judgment, we distinguish three interacting families of axiomatically distinct species: *non-living, living,* and *cognitive.* Among these three, the second, the type known as living processes, is not-entropic relative to the characteristic entropy attributed to non-living process. Relative to all other types of living processes, the human higher cognitive processes stand in the same relationship to other living processes as do living processes generally to non-living phenomena of that macro-scale which is actually or implicitly the domain of sense-perceptions.

The substrate of the interactions between living and non-living processes, is the participation of ostensibly inorganic and other non-living (e.g., organic) material within the processes essential to the continued existence of living processes. Similarly, the cognitive processes of man subsume all living processes, and therefore, also, non-living ones.[8] The coupling of axiomatically living to axiomatically non-living processes, as that link may be represented by the share of an individual phenomenon common to both, illustrates the class of analogous problem which confronts us in examining the coupling of an entropic monetary-financial process to a lawfully not-entropic physical-economic process.

At this moment, all of the nations of the world are dominated by an international regime which is expressed through the agency of the International Monetary Fund. Although the IMF is an institution of United Nations Organization (e.g., world government), it functions as a publicly chartered private corporation, which is in fact a joint-stock-company of the central banking systems of leading powers. These central banks are themselves publicly chartered, but privately held joint-stock companies, which represent leading banks and related financial institutions of their respective nations. The entire system of central banking, the interest which the IMF actually represents, is constructed according to the principles of international monetary and financial practice associated with the London-centered international financier oligarchy. That oligarchy is itself a class of financiers modelled upon the financial nobility of pre-1798, medieval and modern Venice.

This system is a purely entropic one, in which profit appears only in the forms of usury. In other words, the Venice system of usury as profit, belongs to the type which Von Neumann et al. identify as a "zero-sum game": One man's meal is another man's stomach.

As a matter of contrast, a modern physical economy is implicitly a not-entropic process, in which "macroeconomic" profit occurs as "free energy" of a system in which the ratio of "free energy" to "energy of the system" is, modally, always positive. In that latter system, usury, including that of Venice-style monetary-

---

7. The writer has adopted the term "not-entropic," to avoid the cultish use of the term "negentropy" by Prof. Norbert Wiener and his devotees. Wiener, a radical positivist, decrees that "information" in development and communication of ideas, including scientific discoveries of principle, is only an analog for electronic codes transmitted through a medium. On the basis of this assumption, Wiener argues that the gas-theory mathematics of Ludwig Boltzmann's H-theorem applies to the assessment of the idea-content of human communications. To this effect, he employs a less-noticed, included feature of Boltzmann's derivation of his famous H-thereom, the statistical possibility of temporary, local reversals of entropy; Wiener seizes upon this for his assignment of meaning to the term "negative entropy," or "negentropy." Out of the popularization of Wiener's blunder, by the Massachusetts Institute of Technology's Research Lab of Electronics and elsewhere, the popularized dogmas of combined "information theory," "systems analysis," and Korsch-Stalin-Carnap-Russell-Harris-Chomsky "linguistics" have proliferated.

8. We are leaving out of account, as not immediately relevant for this discussion, the suspected sub-atomic, optical-biophysical changes distinguishing inorganic materials participating in living processes, from the same materials encountered in non-living organic material.

financier practices, appears solely a parasitical form, an exacted tribute equal to a needless increase in the percentile of the total economy devoted to merely redundant, or intrinsically useless forms of "general overhead expense."

In all systems of *Family #2*—Quesnay, Smith, Marx, and Von Neumann—profit exists, in fact of practice, only as the looting of either other nations, or of a subordinated large class of persons, or a combination of both. The looting is done by a ruling class, an oligarchy—e.g., feudal aristocracy, London-style financier-merchant nobility, proletarian dictatorship, an "information technocracy"—which imposes and maintains a de facto political dictatorship over both subordinated classes and nations. For all political-economies of this "Family," profit exists only as something extracted by means of usury.

For example, in Volume I of his four-volume **Capital,** and in other places in that four-volume text, Karl Marx states explicitly, that he is leaving out of account the "technological composition of capitals," and the effect of technological progress generally. As a theory of the political-economy of social-reproduction, Marx's entire system breaks down, and becomes, in fact, a theory of profit through usury. This ontological blunder of assumption underlying his **Capital** as a whole, is an important factor in connection with what proved to have been the fatal flaw of the Soviet economic system, the reliance upon what leading Soviet economist Ye. Preobrazhensky had termed "socialist primitive accumulation": the basing of the growth of the Soviet economy as a whole upon the looting of nature, slave labor, and subject nations.[9] As for the usurious model of doctrine and practice of the British economy, had it not existed, for more than two centuries, chiefly as a vora-

---

9. This fatal practice of Soviet "primitive accumulation" may be attributed in part to the costs of military expenditures; more significant, is the high rate of technological progress expressed by the leading edge of the Soviet military-industrial complex, in contrast to the technological sluggishness of the non-military sector, and the lack of the large-scale infrastructure wanted to transform the vastness of the low-population-density Soviet Union into a competitively viable economy. The relevant point here, is that the Soviet system did not accept either the principles of Leibnizian physical economy, or the superiority of the American System of political-economy to the British. Marx's fanatical defense of the "scientific" merit of British political-economy, in his attacks upon the American System of Friedrich List and Henry C. Carey, typify the issue. It was this doctrinal heritage of Marx's anti-scientific anglophilia, which has permeated the socialist movement generally, and which was a conspicuous feature of relevant Soviet official dogma.

cious parasite among nations, it could not have continued long to exist at all.

The pseudo-scientific assertion of some zero-growth ideologues today, that man's relationship to the universe at large is intrinsically entropic, is consistent, as a theory of usury, with the various forms of oligarchical society which are intrinsic to each and all *Family #2* political-economic dogmas. Only political-economies of *Family #1* type are premised functionally upon a not-entropic generation of relative "free energy."

Money and Economy: Temporary 'Peaceful Coexistence'

All competent discussion of the principles of modern economy must begin with attention to a revolution which emerged within Fifteenth-Century Europe. As has been stated in the pages of **EIR** repeatedly, prior to the Fifteenth-Century emergence of a never-previously existing form of society, the modern nation-state, more than 95% of all mankind, in all cultures, had lived as virtual human cattle, in juridical conditions comparable, at best, to serfdom, slavery, or even worse. A brief restatement of that point here, sets the stage for examining the somewhat complex axiomatic heritage which political-economy has acquired during the recent five-and-a-half centuries to date.

An explosive improvement in the condition of man under modern European civilization, began with the complex of developments centered around the A.D. 1438-41 Council of Ferrara-Florence, and the consequent establishment of France in the new form of a "commonwealth," under Louis XI, the new form of sovereign nation-state republic which is the predecessor of our own U.S. Federal Republic of 1789. Inspired, in significant part, by the program of secondary education developed by the Brotherhood of the Common Life, Louis XI's France used the fostering of the creative powers of both orphans and boys from poor strata of the population, as a means of increasing the percentile of the total population capable of assimilating and generating fundamental discoveries of principle in science, Classical art-forms, and technology.

This twofold revolution, the reestablishment of the shattered Catholic Church under the leadership of great figures such as Cardinal Nicolaus of Cusa and Pope Pius II, and the establishment of Louis XI's new-model France as a direct outgrowth of the Council of Florence, redefined the factional division of forces within European civilization and beyond. On the one side, was the emergence of a modern form of sovereign nation-state republic; on the opposing side, the old, usurious forces of the oligarchical tradition, represented chiefly by the financier nobility of Venice, which had emerged, since the beginning of the millennium, as the traditional capital of usurious practices within medieval Europe. Thus, began a five-centuries-long conflict between the forces of good (the modern nation-state republic) and evil (the oligarchical heritage of Venice), which has not been resolved to the present date.

Since the middle of the Eighteenth Century, the paradigm of that conflict between good and evil forms of government, has become the conflict between the American System of political-economy—of Benjamin Franklin, George Washington, Alexander Hamilton, John Quincy Adams, and Abraham Lincoln—and the British monarchy. Britain's domination of the oligarchical forces of this planet, is the crucial issue of the present, systemic breakdown crisis of the world's interconnected monetary and financial systems. This set of circumstances did not come about all at once; knowledge of the history of this development is indispensable for understanding the functioning of the system today. On this account, we summarize the most essential, relevant points identified in earlier editions of **EIR.**

During the Fifteenth and Sixteenth Centuries, the leading opposition to the combined policies of the Council of Florence and of Louis XI's France came from both the Venice-centered financier nobility and the feudal aristocracy. The anti-nation-state alliance of the French feudal aristocrats with Venice, during the course of the Sixteenth, Seventeenth, and Eighteenth Centuries, is typical of the interplay among the sundry opponents of the Council of Florence. The feudalist Clement Prince Metternich's Holy Alliance of 1815-48, is typical of the same type of alliance, then against the influence of the American Revolution, between financier-nobility London and feudal-aristocratic forces of Russia, Austria-Hungary, and elsewhere.

Ultimately, there emerged today's alignments within the oligarchical adversaries of the modern sovereign nation-state institutions: Since the London-directed, Mazzini revolutions of 1848-70, the aristocratic remnants of the Holy Roman Empire and Holy Alliance have been either destroyed through successive revolutions and wars, or assimilated under the leadership of the financier-nobility power centered in the Anglo-Dutch monarchies.

Today, the only significant forces within European civilization, in Europe and the Americas, most notably, are the imperilled heritage of the anti-British, American System of political-economy, and that London-centered oligarchical reaction, the latter which are the heirs of the Venetian, Haileybury tradition of Adam Smith, as represented today by the arch-conspiratorial, fascistic Mont Pelerin Society.

The inability of the oligarchy to destroy the new form of national political-economy, combined with the failure of the new form of political-economy to crush its adversary, the Venice-led oligarchical parasite, established a tragic symbiosis between the two, axiomatically opposed forms of political-economy. In this arrangement, the feudal relics, as long as their power persisted, functioned essentially as auxiliaries of the Venetian, financier-nobility-led faction.[10] Until an extremely radical form of cultural-paradigm shift was introduced, during the interval 1964-72, the financier-nobility was unable to check decisively the impulses of the modern industrialized nation-state, and the political forces of the nation-state-interest were, overall, corrupted into accepting a continued symbiosis with the Venetian parasite and that parasite's superimposed monetary-financial system. In this fashion, the two axiomatically incompatible systems, the American System and the British model of oligarchical central banking, assumed their symbiotic form.

The secret of this prolonged symbiosis is located chiefly in the domain of military and related elements of strategic power.

Until the so-called Pugwash agreements to "Mutual and Assured (thermonuclear) Destruction" (MAD), reached between Moscow and Washington in the aftermath of the 1962 "Cuba Missiles Crisis," London's own designs for maintaining its world-domination depended upon balance-of-power conflicts among London's more powerful rivals. The effect of the 1962-63 agreements reached, partly through the mediation of Bertrand Russell, assured the Anglo-American establishment, notably strategic "utopians" such as National Security Adviser McGeorge Bundy and Secretary of Defense Robert Strange McNamara, that only limited, surrogate warfare was now possible between the two superpowers. In the view of that assessment, the utopian faction within the Western Alliance assumed dom-

---

10. The case of Venice's financing the Habsburg Holy Roman Emperor, Charles V, through the Fuggers, is an example of this Venetian financier-nobility's domination over the European feudal aristocracy.

inance over all policy-shaping, and used that dominance to introduce a fundamental shift in policy: the "post-industrial" and "rock-drug-sex counterculture" shift of the 1964-1972 interval.[11]

From the completion of the scientifically revolutionary cupola of the Florence Cathedral, through the realization of Gottfried Leibniz's design for an industrial development based upon heat-powered machinery, the process leading from the Council of Florence through the emergence and development of the industrialized sovereign nation-state defined an interdependency between per-capita productivity on the one side, and fire-power and mobility of military forces on the other. Thus, from the dissolution of the anti-Venice League of Cambrai, in A.D. 1610, Venice, and later London, maintained its oligarchical power in the face of superior forces, by playing one or more of its adversaries into "balance-of-power" wars against one another. Copying Venice before it, London relied upon establishing its island position as a global financial and maritime power, and playing the second-ranking of its adversaries against the first-ranking.

As long as Britain's power depended upon such "balance of power" warfare, it was impossible to evade altogether the strategic importance of continued productive investment in scientific and technological progress, in basic economic infrastructure, agriculture, mining, manufacturing, construction, and general educational and health policies. As long as the national interests were unwilling to free themselves of the London parasite, the nations were subjected to a division of authority, under which arrangement the national interests developed the physical economy, but the British and allied financier-oligarchical interests controlled the monetary and financial order in the world. Once London and its principal agents were persuaded that "MAD" agreements had eliminated the hazard of general warfare among leading powers, the long-standing tacit agreement between the economic and financier interests was broken: "Post-industrial utopianism" has dominated, increasingly, the trends in world economy and politics, since the assassination of U.S. President John F. Kennedy.

Accordingly, the present worldwide monetary and financial crisis represents chiefly the cumulative impact of two historical legacies from this present century: the 1901-63 policy of commitment to investment in scientific and technological progress, as the means for increasing the productive powers of labor; and, the 1964-95 efforts, to waste and ultimately destroy the agro-industrial-infrastructural base of the modern sovereign nation-state.[12]

This symbiosis, however unwholesome, could be expressed as a relatively peaceful form of relationship between parasite and host, during those moments the physical economy, the host, could produce a greater margin of "macro-economic" profit than was being consumed, as an "income-stream," by the parasite, the superimposed monetary-financial system. Prior to the 1964-72 change, during significant periods, whose duration might be a decade or more, the peace continued, before it was interrupted yet once again, by the social and political effects of so-called cyclical convulsions. Usually, after a period of economic depression, the relative peace was resumed for another decade or so.

The "devil in the detail" of that unwholesome peace between the parasite and host, is the inherent tendency of Venetian-style monetary and financial processes to create fictitious forms of financial capital. It is on this point, this phenomenon, that there appear most clearly and simply the axiomatic differences between the real modern economy of agro-industrial capital and the monetary-financial system of the rentier parasites. In the industrial system, the relative value of any form of capital is determined as the incurred social cost of reproducing a replacement with new real capital of a quality equal to or better than that replaced. In the rentier domain, the matter is quite different; a purely fictitious form of nominal capital may be created by assigning a "market-price" to an income-stream; this is accomplished by selling the title to that expected income- stream at that nominal price: "financial leverage."

Through this parasitical mode of creating fictitious

---

11. One of the typical "markers" for the beginning of that shift was the 1964 publication of a report, **The Triple Revolution,** issued by the Ford Foundation-backed Center for the Study of Democratic Institutions. Following the Ford Foundation-orchestrated events of 1968, the post-industrial shift was effectively completed with such events of 1972 as the post-1971 international monetary conference establishing the speculator's paradise called the "floating exchange-rate" monetary order, and the post-election unleashing of the prepared "Watergate" assault on the institution of the U.S. Presidency.

---

12. It is not required that we document the details of this history here. Only the Rip Van Winkles who went into uninterrupted sleep about Oct. 31, 1963, are not familiar with the 1963-95 countercultural shift as the leading fact of contemporary life.

EIRNS/Stuart Lewis

Nurses march on Washington, March 31, 1995, protesting the gutting of medical services. LaRouche writes, "The paradigm-shift which emerged out of the 1964-72 transition to a 'post-industrial utopia,' impelled the world economy into something quite different than a new cyclical crisis: into the kind of collapse associated with a general breakdown crisis."

capital, "financial leverage," the total nominal capital of such a "mixed economy" may skyrocket far above the actual capital-values of the real economy. To the degree, this burgeoning mass of parasitical fictitious capital seizes control of sections of real estate and the productive sector itself, the result is the so-called "business cycle." However, after the bankrupting of sufficient volumes of the purely fictitious capital, the release of new volumes of agro-industrial production credit, combined with some technology-driver as stimulant, would mobilize a general recovery.

The paradigm-shift which emerged out of the 1964-72 transition to a "post-industrial utopia," impelled the world economy into something quite different than a new cyclical crisis: into the kind of collapse associated with a general breakdown crisis. A glance toward the statistical reports of **EIR**'s John Hoefle, Anthony Wikrent, Christopher White, and their colleagues shows us some of the most crucial of the relevant facts.

Look at this distinction in "macro-economic" terms. In the pre-1964 form of symbiosis between the two axiomatically distinct systems, the revenues of financial capital were derived, in net, from a portion of the operating profit of agro-industrial production as a whole. Through the mechanisms of industrial banking, and related modes of credit-flow into the productive sector of the economy, finance-capital maintained and enhanced its gross revenue, without significantly increasing its share of the operating profit of that productive sector. That was the precondition for the "peaceful coexistence" of the host and its rentier parasite.

Increase capital-intensity in an energy-intensive mode, and, all the while, maintain and build up extensive works in water-management, in power generation and distribution, in integrated modern transport and warehousing systems, in better communications, in improved public primary, secondary, and higher education, in investments in generating scientific and technological progress, and in improving the longevity and productivity of the population through improved health-care. These were, and are still, the preconditions for increasing the net, "macro-economic" productive powers of labor. That is the only way in which the Federal budget could ever be balanced. Those were the watch-words of progress and prosperity, which made the United States of America the world's most awesome economic success, prior to the 1964-72 cultural-paradigm shift.

Look at the results of Christopher White's expressing the official statistics in terms of market-baskets of consumption and production, per capita, per household, and per unit of land-area utilized (**Figures 1** and **2**). Since the high-point of about 1967-69, the standard of consumption for households, by category of productively employed wage-earner, has collapsed continuously. That is, if we measure the beans and bacon, clothing, housing, quality of education, and so forth, which that wage-earner's income may purchase, the American employed in productive occupations has become poorer and poorer during the course of the recent 25 years to date. The per-capita productivity of the total U.S. labor-force, as measured in the contents of the same market-baskets of combined household and agro-industrial consumptions, has also been declining over the same period. In fact, as measured in real, rather than financial terms, the U.S. economy has been operat-

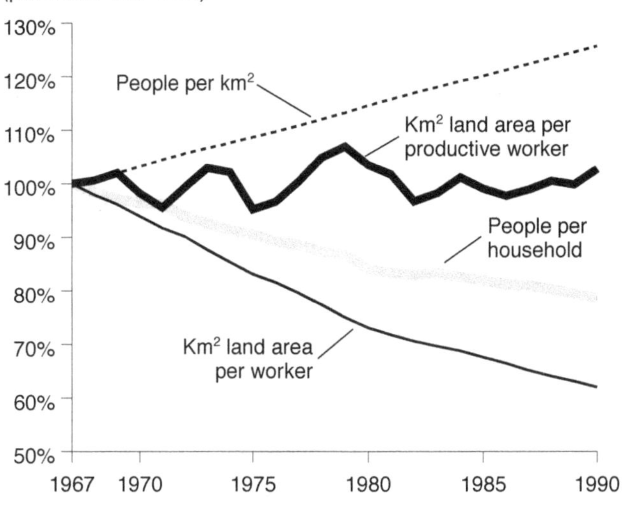

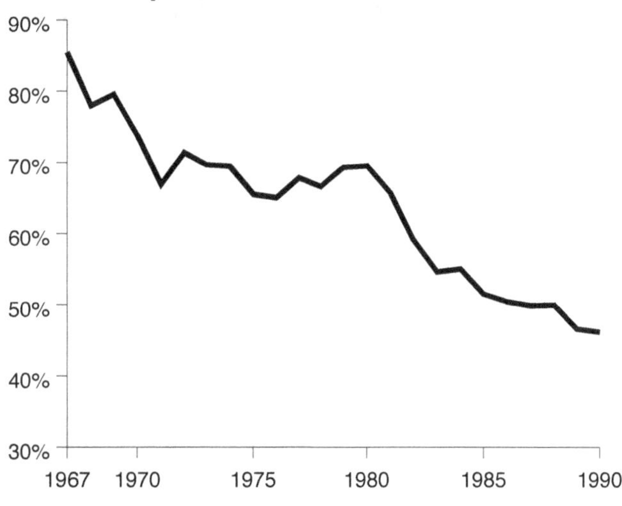

ing at a net loss over the past 25 years.

However, during that same 25 years, since 1970-71, the U.S. financial economy has grown, approximately hyperbolically, over the same period the real economy has been in an accelerating collapse. The $64 trillions question: Is this a mere statistical coincidence, or is the cause of growth of financial aggregates also the cause for the collapse of the real economy? Is the continued existence of *Family #2,* the entropic Adam Smith model, the cause for the spiral of collapse of the *Family #1* process, the real economy? Has the "Adam Smith model" become the malignant cancer which must be removed soon, if the host, the real economy, is to survive?

The answer is, "Yes." The growing size of the income-stream, from the real economy, upon which the parasite depends to survive, is the margin by which the rate of collapse is increased in the already negative-profit real economy. The fact that the survival of the speculative financial bubble of fictitious capital depends upon destroying the same real economy upon which the existence of the bubble depends, demonstrates that the present crisis is a systemic one, not a mere financial collapse, but a general breakdown crisis, leading toward the disintegration of existing monetary and financial institutions.

The peace between the parasite and host is now a thing of the past, forever.

The lack of peace, is a state of war. This war is not an abstract one; it is an actual war between the British monarchy, the political embodiment of the global parasite, on the one side, and the leading real-economy of the world, the United States, on the other. The power of the London-centered international oligarchy is chiefly its domination of the world through the financial power gathered around the International Monetary Fund and World Bank. That financial political power of the London-centered oligarchy, is being destroyed by this collapse: the distress of the London Warburg banking house, and the collapse of Baring's and Lloyd's, typify the ongoing destruction of the majority of the financial pillars of the British monarchy itself. In this case, the "continuation of politics by other means" signifies, as we see, more and more, day by day, the shift from political-financial means, to such "other means" as the London-orchestrated Balkan wars and the escalation of international terrorism, even into the United States itself.

Why Most Taught 'Economics' Is a Fraud

The fraud inhering in the taught economics of virtually all university classrooms today, reflects a series of ultimately related but distinct blunders of underlying assumption. These frauds not only dominate the university classroom; they are the frauds permeating the work of most Nobel Prize for Economics recipients. They have had a disastrous effect through their hegemony in the policymaking of governmental and leading private economic institutions throughout most of the world today.

EIRNS/Christopher Lewis

Friends of Lyndon LaRouche, members of the Civil Rights Movement Solidarity, campaign in a state election in North Rhine-Westphalia, Germany, August 1995. The poster reads: "Down with Asininity! Economic Construction, Not Financial Collapse."

in its whole, as a social and political phenomenon, the British oligarchy of today, is a typical product of this Aristotelean heritage.

However, the Aristotelean heritage of the British monarchy, is of a special sub-type: the "neo-Aristotelean" followers of the majority faction within late-Sixteenth-, Seventeenth-, and Eighteenth-Centuries' Venice, the faction of Paolo Sarpi, the faction which created the Anglo-Dutch monarchy. Sarpi, the actual founder of modern, neo-Aristotelean empiricism and its positivist outgrowth, was the patron of such signal figures of England's early Seventeenth Century as Francis Bacon and Galileo Galilei; Thomas Hobbes was a shared asset of Bacon and Galileo. René Descartes is of the same genre, as are all of the British, French, and Austo-Hungarian empiricists, positivists, and existentialists, down through the present day's university classrooms.[15]

That dogma of British empiricism is the source of the principal, explicit fraud of virtually all generally accepted, "quackademic" varieties of today's university-classroom economics today.[16] The center of that fraud,

Some of the blunders, in axiom and method, underlying those teachings, are special to the empiricist "social science" upon which taught economics, including Von Neumann's "systems analysis," is explicitly based. Others are adopted from the influence of the Hobbes-Locke doctrine of "human nature" upon the gnostic theological assumptions underlying the mechanistic mathematical physics of Galileo Galilei, René Descartes, Isaac Newton, LaPlace, Clausius-Kelvin, Helmholtz, and the modern radical positivists. To understand the present problem adequately, take a moment to dissect those principal such influences responsible for the pervasive incompetence of virtually everything taught as "economics" in the university classroom today.[13]

The common root of these hoaxes is the continuing influence, today, of the savagely incompetent, pro-oligarchical counter-method, which Aristotle developed, in his hysterical effort to discredit, and eradicate the scientific method of the recently deceased Plato.[14] Taken

---

13. On Galileo, et al., see Lyndon H. LaRouche, Jr., "'Structures of Sin' Still Rule the Nations," **EIR,** April 28, 1995, pp. 46-56.

14. During the period from Solon's anti-oligarchical, anti-usury reforms at Athens, through and beyond the death of Plato, the fundamental issue at the birth of European civilization, was the conflict between the republican principle of Solon, Socrates, and Plato, versus the Persian/oligarchical "model" of the Babylonian Empire continued under the Achaemenid dynasty. Aristotle, a trained sophist, and protégé and spy of both King Philip of Macedon and Isocrates' School of Rhetoric at Athens, was an adherent of the oligarchical method. This advocacy is demonstrated most luridly in his **Ethics** and his **Politics,** and his writings on metaphysics and method generally.

15. See, LaRouche, "'Structures of Sin'…," *op. cit.*

16. The author and his associates first employed the neologism "quackademic" in post-August 15th 1971, to designate generally accepted classroom economics of that time (and, still today). The occasion for use of this neologism, then, was the Aug. 15-16, 1971 breakdown of the Bretton Woods monetary system, which every leading U.S. economist, excepting this writer, had proclaimed to be impossible. At that time, in response to this writer's charges on this account, a senior Keynesian economist, Distinguished Professor Abba Lerner, was selected as the champion, to defend the economics profession against this writer's charges of pervasive academic and other professional incompetence in this field. In the conclusion of that public

EIRNS/Stuart Lewis

Organizing on the streets of Washington, D.C., March 1995, for Lyndon LaRouche's economic recovery program, and against the "quackademic" economists.

is the irrationalist teaching, that economic policies must be determined by "the market."

Had modern Europe and North America tolerated that nonsense-demand during earlier centuries, the world would still be less than 400 millions poor souls, over 90% wallowing in the impoverished, brutish illiteracy of serfdom or worse. Mankind would never have escaped from the murderous bonds of feudal servitude, Venetian usury, and even such more inhuman conditions of bestiality as Aztec rule. If we follow in the pol-

icies of Mont Pelerin Society ideologies, such as Newt Gingrich's "Contract with America," or irrationalist fanatics such as Sen. Phil Gramm, we shall rediscover the utopian conditions of pre-A.D. 1400 feudalism and barbarism, all too soon.

All of today's generally accepted university-classroom economics dogma, purports to explain the secrets of the not-entropic growth of the modern agro-industrial nation-state economy, from the standpoint of the ruling axiomatic assumptions of an entropic, linear system of pairwise truck-and-barter, all conducted under a regime of Venice-modelled system of usury. To define a putative model of modern society, these fellows borrow shamelessly, as the principal axiom of their systems, the same *laissez-faire* which Dr. Quesnay concocted to prescribe the non-interference of both government and urban institutions contrary to the empyreal prudence of the class of parasites known as feudal aristocrats. That is the same *laissez-faire* which Adam Smith plagiarized from Quesnay, as what today's victims of the mass-murderous IMF might fairly and bitterly describe as Smith's universal snake-oil remedy, "free trade."[17]

All of today's "quackademic" economists premise their views and method upon one or another species from among *Family #2* theorem-lattices: e.g., treat "macroeconomic" profit as an epiphenomenon of a "Bounty of Nature," or "Bounty of Trade," and so on. To wit: They deny the existence of an efficient expression of an individual's human creative powers of reason. So-called "information theory" and "systems analysis" are only more extreme, and much cruder than the celebrated German empiricist Immanuel Kant on

---

debate, on New York City's Queens College campus, Lerner blurted out a confession of the accuracy of this writer's charges, that liberal economists would now move to promote fascistic forms of austerity against developing nations and others, modelled upon the practice of Nazi Economics Minister Hjalmar Schacht. Now, the post-1987 acceleration of the speculative avalanche in "derivatives," creates an analogous situation for most Nobel-Prize-winning and other professional economists; once again, most of them have been exposed by events, as "quackademics."

17. Compare "'Structures of Sin'...," *op. cit.,* pp. 49-50, 53-56, on Bernard Mandeville, Adam Smith, and Galileo Galilei. Mandeville's 1725 "Private Vices, Public Benefits" gives away the secret of *laissez-faire,* "free trade," and the modern "Chaos Theory" of Ilya Prigogine, et al. Mandeville is also echoing Thomas Hobbes and John Locke: the argument that the random, pairwise interaction of evil individual impulses and acts converges asymptotically upon the production of the public good. Smith underscores this by explicitly advocating his employer's, the British East India Company's destruction of peoples, such as those of China, through traffic in opium, just as his devotee, Prof. Milton Friedman, has endorsed that drug-epidemic which has made the U.S. population (according to U.S. government reports of convictions and incarcerations) the most criminally inclined population of any nation upon this planet today. Might we not thus suspect that Mandeville's dogma—along with the "chaos theory" of Hobbes, Locke, and Adam Smith—might have been savagely disproven by the failure of Milton Friedman's little experiment?

this point.[18] The issue is as old as the reductionist Eleatic school's attack on Pythagoras,[19] Aristotle's attacks upon Plato, and Kant's attacks upon Leibniz. In their radical expression, these attacks insist that valid *ideas,* as Plato defines ideas, do not exist, apart from those derived from sense-certainty. In the alternative, like Kant in his own "Critiques," the notable opponents of Plato, Nicolaus of Cusa,[20] Leonardo da Vinci, Johannes Kepler, and of Gottfried Leibniz, have always insisted that if "intuitions" of such ideas might exist, new creations of that sort cannot be objects of intelligible fore-knowledge.

All of these modern opponents of science were followers of Venice's teachers of Aristoteleanism. They are divided into two groupings, the first, the earlier, "stay south" grouping of Pietro Pomponazzi, Gasparo Contarini, Francesco Zorzi, et al., and the "strike north" Venice faction of the founders of British empiricism and, later, Kantianism, Paolo Sarpi, et al. This continuing, ancient dispute respecting the existence and nature of *ideas,* is, axiomatically, the crucial practical issue of political-economy today.

During the recent months, the present writer has adopted the famous measurement of the length of the Earth's meridian by Plato Academy member and Archimedes contemporary, Eratosthenes,[21] as the model pedagogy which might be used for demonstrating to secondary pupils, among others, the existence of Platonic "ideas." The relevant features of that measurement, are, summarily, as follows.

Suppose that two somewhat distant locations in ancient, Ptolemaic Egypt, Alexandria and Syene (Aswan), lie upon the same, astronomically determined North-South line, a common meridian. Measure the distance along that common line between the two points. Then, construct two duplicate sundials, as follows (**Figure 3**). Construct a hemispherical shell. In the "South Pole" of this shell, pointing (by aid of a plumb-bob) to the center of the Earth, insert a straight stick, along the extended line implicitly defined by the plumb-bob. Around the inside rim of the hemisphere, mark off gradations; at the points the Earth's meridian will intersect the rim of that hemisphere, draw the half of a great circle passing through the South Pole of the hemisphere; mark points of gradation along this line. Set one of these hemispheres in place in Syene, the other in Alexandria.

As each of the two sundials shows high noon, measure the angle which the stick's shadow casts along the semi-circle passing through the South Pole. Observe, then, that the angle of the shadow cast in Alexandria differs from the angle of the shadow cast in Syene. Given the fact that the distance between the South

---

18. Since most recent university teaching on the subject of Kant and his work is virtually illiterate, the following footnote on the historical position, and present-day relevance of Kant's doctrines, is supplied. Kant, born in 1724, became, approximately 1740-44, a collateral asset of the networks of Venice's spy-master Abbot Antonio Conti, closely tied to Conti's networks within Frederick the Great's anti-Leibniz Berlin Academy (Academy member Gotthold Lessing was a rare exception among Conti's anti-Leibniz crew of Maupertuis, Voltaire, Algarotti, Euler, et al.). The most notable early influence upon Kant during the early period was the influential specialist in bowdlerized, Aristotelean interpretations of Leibniz, the Newton devotee Christian Wolff. After that, he was strongly influenced by another product of the Conti-Voltaire network of salons, the pathetic Jean-Jacques Rousseau. During the middle of the 1760s through the middle of the 1770s, Kant became a devotee of empiricist David Hume. As Kant emphasizes in his apologia, the 1783 **Prolegomena to a Future Metaphysic,** his 1781 **Critique of Pure Reason** was a break, not with the young Hume, but the aged Hume who had turned from early-Eighteenth-Century empiricism, to what became known as "Nineteenth-Century British philosophical radicalism," the radical empiricism of Adam Smith, Jeremy Bentham et al. Kant remained a mid-Eighteenth-Century empiricist to the end of his life (e.g., his 1790 **Critique of Judgment**). The rampant philosophical irrationalism of his last "Critique" became the virtual "bible" of the Nineteenth-Century German Romantic movement, of Karl Savigny, Franz Liszt, Richard Wagner, and other prophets of Twentieth-Century conservative-fascist currents in existentialism. For a prophetic insight into Kant, and Kant's fascistic tendencies, see Heinrich Heine, **The Romantic School** (1835), and **On the History of Religion and Philosophy in Germany** (1835). It was the radical positivism growing largely out of Nineteenth-Century "neo-Kantian" Romanticism, which turns up as the crucial axiomatic feature of both Prof. Norbert Wiener's pathetic "information theory," and the axiomatically correlated "systems analysis" of John Von Neumann.

19. I.e., according to Plato. See his **Parmenides.**

20. The principal attacks upon Cardinal Nicolaus of Cusa, since those of the reductionist Wenck, have been focussed against Cusa's use of Socratic method (e.g., **De docta ignorantia=On Learned Ignorance**) to found modern science. The forerunner of British empiricism was the relatively wide circulation in England of Venice agent Francesco Zorzi's attack, **Harmonia Mundi,** on Cusa's method of *docta ignorantia.* Cusa, in addition to being the leading agent of the Vatican in bringing about the 1438-41 Council of Ferrara-Florence, was the most important influence upon the development of modern science, via such self-avowed students of his work as Luca Pacioli, Leonardo da Vinci, and Johannes Kepler. An English translation of Wenck's attack and Cusa's response is found in **Nicholas of Cusa's Debate With John Wenck,** Jasper Hopkins, trans. (Minneapolis, Minn.: The Arthur J. Banning Press, 1984.)

21. See **Greek Mathematical Works,** Ivor Thomas, trans. (London: Harvard University Press/William Heineman, Ltd., 1941), Vol. II, pp. 266-273. Eratosthenes' construction is being replicated currently in Europe, as a demonstration experiment for use in secondary-level educational programs.

Eratosthenes' Method for Measuring the Size of the Earth

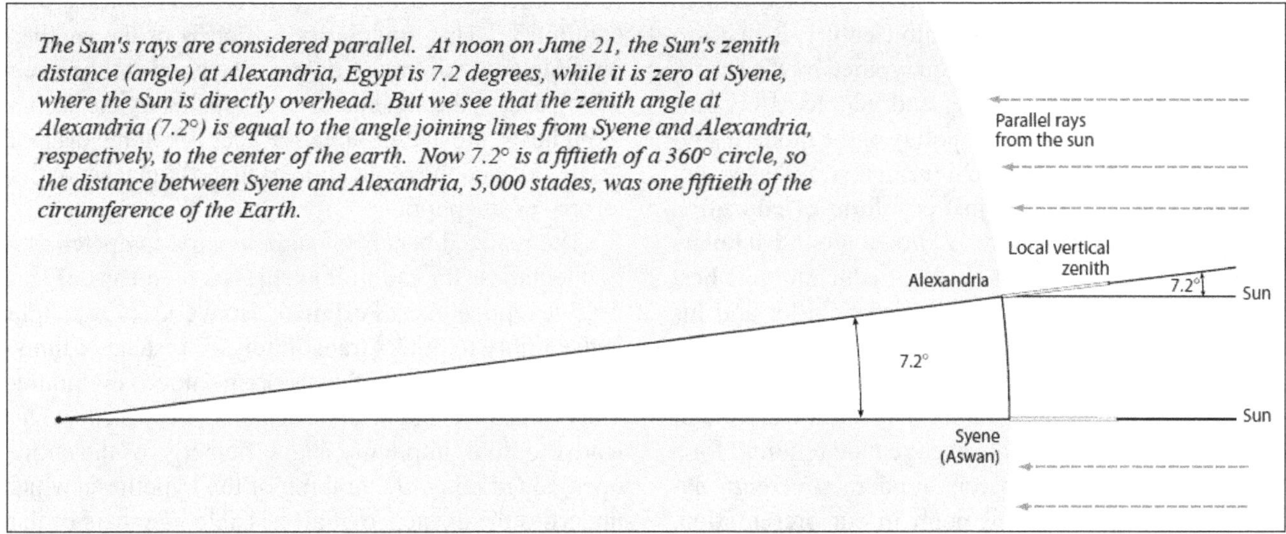

Poles of the two sundials is known, and the respective angles of the shadows, the estimated polar diameter of the Earth—to an accuracy within approximately 50 miles—follows, without trigonometry, by construction.

In the usual case such an experiment were presented, the most crucial lesson to be learned would be brushed over without attention. What must not be brushed over, is this: *How was it possible, that Eratosthenes could have measured, with such remarkable relative accuracy, a curvature of the Earth which no man was to have seen until 2,200 years later?* What Eratosthenes did observe with his senses, was not the curvature of the Earth, but, rather, an anomalous difference in two sense-perceptions: the difference in the angles cast by the respective shadows. Once that later qualification is made, we have defined the point at which we depart the realm of what is no more than useful engineering, to enter the realm of science.

All science, as distinct from the valuable, although inferior realm of engineering, is defined, not by ideas associated within sense-perception, but, rather, by the ideas which are generated by anomalies which appear to destroy the authority of sense-perception as such.

Consider related cases from the scientific achievements of Plato's Academy and its collaborators. Consider the case, that, before Eratosthenes' discoveries, at an earlier point during the Third Century B.C., Aristarchus had demonstrated that the Earth orbits the Sun—although, from the Second Century A.D., until Nicolaus of Cusa, Copernicus, and Kepler, official Europe is reputed to have believed the deliberate, Aristotelean fraud perpetrated by Claudius Ptolemy, the lying assertion that the universe orbited the Earth. Consider the approximate measurement of the distance between the Earth and the Moon, by Eratosthenes, and others, when no man had seen that distance with his senses. These examples each and all typify the fact that every scientific discovery of principle, from before Thales, through to the present time, involves the generation of an *idea,* in Plato's sense of "idea," an idea which is derived from anti-Aristotelean, *anti-empiricist* cognition of an anomaly among sense-perceptions, which contradicts naive sense-perception. All scientific ideas, and the crucial ideas of Classical forms of art, are of this Platonic quality.

The principles of political-economy are of this efficient quality. By "efficient," one should signify that these are ideas which are the cause of mankind's increase of society's power over nature, per capita, per household, and per unit-area of land employed. It is these ideas which are the efficient agency through which the average productive powers of labor are increased. This is the efficient means, by which the output of human activity of societies as a whole exceeds the input required to generate and sustain that activity. This is the source of not-entropy in economy, the source of sustainable, and also rising rates of "macro-economic" profit.

Education and Profit

The secret of the great advance in society which erupted during Europe's Fifteenth Century, is that impulse toward universal education typified by the Brotherhood of the Common Life, and adopted by Louis XI's France as a cornerstone-policy of the modern sovereign nation-state. This achievement was based not upon the goal of making just any form of education universal, but, rather, what is known among scholars as the Classical-humanist mode of education, as best typified by the policies of Friedrich Schiller and his follower, Prussia's famous education minister, Wilhelm von Humboldt. The Humboldt model of gymnasium as a secondary institution, is the best example of the kind of policy of universal education required for a future citizen of a prosperous modern sovereign nation-state republic. At this point in our presentation, the most crucial features of that educational policy, as they bear upon the product of profit, may be stated briefly, as follows.

We begin with the direct impact of scientific progress upon the "macro-economic" profitability of national economies. After that, we identify the relevance of education in Classical art-forms to the same effect.

The principles of a Classical-humanist form of scientific education are summarized as follows. The distinction of this form of science-education, is that it demands that currently prevalent "textbook" and other "blab-school" methods of education be abandoned, in favor of the proposition, that the pupil has no actual knowledge, except to the degree that the pupil has re-experienced the act of an original scientific or artistic discovery of principle, within his or her own mental processes. The function of the teachers is to prepare the pupils for each such experience, within a succession of such experiences, which may be fairly described as arranged in the sequence of "necessary predecessor," "necessary successor."

In the language of formal mathematical physics, the state of consistent knowledge, prior to discovery of a superior principle, is represented by an open-ended theorem-lattice. That lattice is premised upon a set of stated or implied formal axioms, which, taken as an integrated set, constitute what Plato defines as an *hypothesis.* The validated, newly discovered, higher principle, defines a new, relatively superior *hypothesis.* No theorem of the first hypothesis is consistent with any theorem of the second hypothesis; this formal inconsistency is otherwise recognizable as a *singularity* of the general form otherwise associated with a "mathematical discontinuity." That singularity, which is of the smallest possible non-zero magnitude, corresponds to the event which causes the supersession of the first by the second hypothesis, the mental-creative act of both the original discovery, and the replication of that original act of discovery by the pupil.

The realized benefit of rudimentary competence in mathematics (for example) achieved by means of successive replications of original discoveries of principle, is the ability to think "transfinitely."[22] Instead of thinking of the elements of a theorem-lattice, or kindred array of many elements, one at a time, in sequence: One learns to think implicitly, and efficiently, of the entire, open-ended array, by thinking of the hypothesis which underlies the existence of all possible members of that array. It may be fairly said, that that pupil has made the initial transition to thinking "axiomatically."

Through the successive replication of original discoveries in that way, the pupil acquires a still-higher level of knowledge, above the level of simply "thinking axiomatically." Through this kind of mental experience, repeated many times, the pupil is confronted with the fact, that underlying a succession of demonstrably valid historical discoveries of principle, there is an associated, implied *method of discovery,* corresponding to Plato's notion of an *higher hypothesis.* This is the level of thinking which Johannes Kepler, for example, identifies by his notion of a governing principle of *Reason* in the laws of the universe.[23]

This acquired level of transfinite thinking[24] which enables the pupil to render intelligible the notion of localized process-interaction among different axiomatic systems, is the level required for making intelligible the crucial characteristics of modern economies, or for rendering comprehensible an historical process of revolutionary scientific discoveries of principle.

To the degree that the action of thought of an individual person incorporates an accumulation of a relatively greater number of axiomatic-revolutionary dis-

---

22. This is the sense of "transfinite" employed by Georg Cantor.

23. As distinct from the Sarpi-Galileo-Newton notion of mechanical "causality." See Lyndon H. LaRouche, Jr., "The Fraud of Algebraic Causality," **Fidelio,** Winter 1994.

24. This higher quality of "transfiniteness," is what Georg Cantor associates with Plato's notion of a *Becoming,* as distinct from the higher ontological state of Cantor's *Absolute* or Plato's *Good.*

coveries, we may say that the density of discontinuities per interval of action is increased. This is not merely verbal action, but also efficient action by the individual upon nature, and so forth. These phenomena are located in the Platonic quality of non-empiricist "ideas," within such ideas as "efficient ideas."

The accumulation of knowledge in this form, through all of the many things which are transmitted to the infant and child as a "cultural heritage," is the correlative of those increases in mankind's potential relative population-density which set the individual member of the human species absolutely apart from, and absolutely above the members of all other species. This is the quality which is responsible for the increase of the human population, and its demographic parameters of life-expectancy, health, and productivity, orders of magnitude above the "aboriginal food-gathering" potential attributable to higher apes.

This notion of increase of the density of such discontinuities per interval of mental action, is the formal correlative of the not-entropy of political economy. This is the source of "macro-economic" profit. This is the origin of the capability of the ratio of "free energy" to "energy of the system," to remain constant or to rise, while the "energy of the system," per capita, per household, and per unit of land-area utilized, increases.

The origin of this benefit is not limited to science education, or any part of education as such, but, nonetheless, Classical-humanist education, as we have described it here, thus far, is paradigmatic of all of those developments within society which bring about the desired, not-entropic result. It is the increase of the ration of the educated strata of society, from less than 5% of the population, in the direction of universal, Classical-humanist modes of education of the young, which accounts both for the explosion of growth of productivity, and for the general improvement in the condition of humanity, unleashed by the Fifteenth-Century Council of Florence and Louis XI's France.

As soon as the principle of "efficient knowledge" is formulated in such Classical-humanist terms, we ought to recognize, and quickly, that there is an inhering fraud in today's popular use of the terms "objective science" and "scientific objectivity." Those uses of "objective" flow from Aristotle and his co-religionists among the modern materialists, empiricists, and positivists.[25] They

signify acceptance of the popularized delusion, that valid ideas are limited to the objects one may presume to be reflected as sense-perceptions. The fact—the relevant anomaly—is, that were science "objective" in the sense the materialists and empiricists prescribe, the living human population of this planet never would have exceeded the several millions individuals imputable to an "aboriginal" collection of ape-like food-gatherers.

The case of Classical-humanist science-education underlines the fact that valid scientific knowledge is essentially subjective. Science pertains to those ideas which meet two essential requirements: that they are not reflections of sense-perceptions as such, but, rather, arise as creative solutions to stubborn anomalies in sense-perception; it is also required, secondly, that their superior efficiency is demonstrable in social practice. The general form of the latter requirement is, that the demographic characteristics of populations be improved, and that the potential relative population-density of mankind is implicitly increased, relative to the surface of our home planet. These ideas occur as products of a uniquely-human creative potential of the individual mind, and are governed by a still-higher quality of idea, above ordinary hypothesis, higher hypothesis, or scientific method.

The case for the Classical art-forms (poetry, drama, music, plastic fine arts), is of a related form. In art, the place of singularities in science education is taken by *metaphor*. The principles of creative discovery in Classical fine art are the same as for valid discovery of superior principles in science.

It is the combination of the two, Classical-humanist modes of scientific education, and Classical-humanist education in the fine arts, which defines the roundly developed young personality of a good modern culture, the suitable citizen of a sovereign nation-state republic.

It is the subjective qualities of developed powers of creative discovery in science and fine arts, which define both areas of knowledge: knowledge is not "objective"; it is "subjective."

The essential lesson of the whole experience of modern European civilization, in both its rise, 1461-1963, and its recent slide toward collapse, 1964-95, is that the essential investment, upon which the "macroeconomic" profitability, and even the bare survival of modern nations depends, is investment in the development and utilization of the creative powers of the indi-

---

25. Is not atheism (or Thomas Huxley's "agnosticism") also a religion?

vidual person, as we have described that creativity summarily, here. There is no possible equilibrium-state in an econmy; to maintain not-entropic progress of society, even its mere survival, the process of not-entropic development through the fruits of creative-mental discovery, must continue. Heraclitus observed, "Nothing is constant, but change." "Change" is not-entropic development.

The Interaction

Against the elements of background so arrayed, let us restate and analyze the crucial decision presently confronting the governments of the world's nations today.

Beginning with tremors of a coming financial "mudslide," in 1992, there has been a remorseless, hyperbolic growth in the numbers and severity of bankruptcies and near-bankruptcies associated with the threatened bursting of a global bubble of financial speculation in so-called "derivatives."[26] By early 1995, the "mudslide" had become mammoth in scale, a global epidemic. The policy-question posed by the latter developments is fairly summed up by those now preparing their participation in the coming Halifax monetary conference: "It *is* a global epidemic! Does the collapse represent a set of administrative blunders, or is it a systemic crisis which augurs the early end of the international monetary system in its present institutional form?"

The answer is, the ongoing collapse *is* the onrush of an inevitable end of the present form of global monetary and financial system. No mere improvement in administration or administrative procedures would have any significant benefit. There is no solution, but that at least several leading governments take the initiative in putting the existing monetary system into financial-bankruptcy reorganization, to clear the way for the prompt establishment of a new international credit system, one based upon the precedent of the highly successful national banking established under the administration of U.S. President George Washington.

If that bankruptcy-reform is not made relatively soon, the existing system will disintegrate in a global echo of the 1922-23 disintegration of the monetary system of Weimar Germany. The "virus" which would then obliterate the present global monetary and financial order, was endemic to the system even before 1963. However, as the Franklin Roosevelt war-time mobilization demonstrated, as long as the potential for resuming net physical growth in the agro-industrial sectors of physical production existed, it were possible to revive a virtually comatose monetary and financial system, through the combined current and prediscountable, future real profits of agriculture, industry, and infrastructure-building.

From the standpoint of comparison to the 1931-45 U.S. economy, we have reached the present stage, at which no such recovery of the monetary and financial system would be possible: The difference is, for the greater part of 30 years, and emphatically the past 25, we have allowed the destruction of the nation's physical-productive capacity and skilled labor-force to go much too far, for too long. The accumulated financial debts of the world could never be repaid under the existing system, or anything like it. To survive, we must scrap the sick system, and begin over once again.

It will do our opponents no good to argue against this picture. Either the system will be reformed radically, in bankruptcy, along the lines I have indicated, or the system will disintegrate. There is no way in which the opponents of that radical reform could win the argument. Here, we are addressing a different aspect of the problem. "Objectively," as some might say, the successful reorganization of the world's economy is within reach; there is no technical reason it should not succeed, provided the indicated changes in axiomatic policies are made. The danger to be considered, is that, even after the dying present system has gone bankrupt, the mental habits—the axiomatic assumptions—associated with the departed system will persist. For that reason, it is of vital strategic interest to every nation of the world, the United States included, that the reputations of today's generally accepted university-classroom economics doctrines be destroyed.

In conclusion, therefore, we summarize the method of thinking about political-economy which must be rejected, and what must be affirmed in its place. The contrast between the Eighteenth Century's so-called "Robinson-Crusoe model," the linear, entropic method, as resurrected by John Von Neumann and Oskar Morgenstern for their 1943 **Theory of Games and Economic**

---

26. See John Hoefle, "Derivatives: The Last Gasp of the Speculative Bubble," **EIR,** April 14, 1995.

Behavior[27], versus the scientific method exemplified by Bernhard Riemann's 1854 habilitation dissertation, "On the Hypotheses Which Underlie Geometry," which we referenced here, earlier.

As if emulating the opening chapters of Karl Marx's four-volume **Capital,** Von Neumann and Morgenstern introduce the fictional image of Robinson Crusoe and Friday, as the idealized "cell-form" of their entire system of economic values. There is nothing intrinsically human in Von Neumann's and Morgenstern's ideal economic man, barring such superficial aping as a bit of crude tool-making, barter, and casino gambling. There is no rational basis for the choices in the trade between Robinson and Friday; there are only varying relative intensities of desires. All is an n-person game involving m varieties of articles traded and consumed, in varying degrees of absolute or relative finitude: Begin with a two-person game, and proceed from there. Apparently, nothing is involved which can not be presented for mathematical solutions as a system of simultaneous linear inqualities. The system is intrinsically entropic.

Modern systems analysis is, arguably, conceptually cruder than many among its notable predecessors, but, in principle, it exemplifies all *Family #2* species. These entropic "models" are in stunning contrast to Riemann's principle of hypothesis, the principle which bears directly upon the crucial fact of physical economy.

Riemann's habilitation dissertation does not define a geometry in the ordinary sense. Rather, classroom Euclidean geometry is not a true reflection of the physical space-time in which we live, nor is it a direct reflection of the evidence taken by our visual apparatus. Euclidean geometry is a construction of the naive imagination. In classroom Euclidean geometry, we merely imagine that space-time is extended without limit, and in perfect continuity, in the directions of backwards-forward, side-to-side, and up-down in space, and backwards-forwards in time: This is not true in vision, for example, in which space is harmonically ordered, and is not perfectly continuous in any sense of direction. Riemann addresses the point, that if we attempt to impose the results of validated discoveries in physics upon the Euclidean image of space-time, we are presented with some provocative, and very useful anoma-

lies. This may be summed up in the following way, for our purposes here.

The human mind may imagine many things which we do not know from prior experience. Some of these imagined ideas prove to be states which can be discovered, or induced in nature; more cannot. The significant, valid imaginations of this sort are discoveries of the type which the referenced Eratosthenes experiment illustrates. They are discoveries of physical principle which contradict earlier conceptions of physical space-time, but which nonetheless prove to be valid. Discoveries of this type demand a change in hypothesis. The interesting thing to discover, then, is: What method of discovery (e.g., "Family" of discoveries) subsumes the relevant series of valid crucial discoveries of this valid type?

What then, is the result of the attempt to correct our notion of geometry in a way which reflects this notion? That is the general idea one should associate with the term "Riemannian geometries" in particular, or "non-Euclidean geometry" in general. This is the form of geometry which lies beyond the bounds of all ordinary notions of a formalist mathematics; this is the appropriate geometry for a valid idea of "physical space-time." This is the appropriate geometry for representing the physical-space-time of a not-entropic physical-economic process.

In this physical-economic "geometry," our attention is focussed upon the interaction of physical-economic processses which are defined as axiomatically mutually exclusive: a succession of interacting economic "geometries" which act upon one another in such a fashion as to raise the state of the subject economy from a relatively lower to a relatively higher degree of not-entropy. The paradigm for this interaction is the Classical-humanist method in education: the development, in the individual, of the creative power for assimilating and generating (Platonic qualities of) ideas which represent valid creative discoveries of physical and artistic principle. It is the transmission of those ideas, in that manner, which is the concrete form of the interaction to which we have just referred here: It is called otherwise, the fostering of scientific and artistic progress in both the generation and efficient assimilation to practice of valid discoveries of higher principle.

The difference is: It is no mere epiphenomenon of bad metaphysics: It is real, and intelligibly so.

---

27. Third edition (Princeton, N.J.: Princeton University Press, 1953).